SPARE THE ROD AND
SPOIL THE CHURCH

SPARE THE ROD AND SPOIL THE CHURCH

Donald Bridge

A ministry of World Vision

MARC
EUROPE

MARC Europe is an integral part of World Vision, an international Christian humanitarian organisation. MARC's object is to assist Christian leaders with factual information, surveys, management skills, strategic planning and other tools for evangelism. We also publish and distribute related books on mission, church growth, management, spiritual maturity and other topics.

British Library Cataloguing in Publication Data

Bridge, Donald
    Spare the rod and spoil the church.
    1. Church discipline
    I. Title
    262.9   LAW
    ISBN 0–947697–10–1

Typeset by Creative Editors & Writers Ltd. Printed in Great Britain for MARC Europe, Cosmos House, 6 Homesdale Road, Bromley, Kent BR2 9EX by Cox & Wyman Ltd., Cardiff Road, Reading, Berks RG1 8EX.

Contents

Acknowledgements

Writing a book far from home is not an easy task. I want to express my special thanks to those who have helped me with typing and practical support: Mrs Pat Morgan, secretary to the Anglican Bishop of Jerusalem; Mrs Daphne Waelend and Mrs Joyce Bell, members of the staff of the Garden Tomb; and my wife Rita. Thank you!

Jerusalem, 1985

Part One: The Precepts

CHAPTER ONE

The Forgotten Factor

IN my mind, it all began with two bishops.

Both of them made the newspaper headlines. One of them sacked an ordained church officer who was having an affair with a member of his parish. Journalistic comment was divided. Secular papers expressed incredulity and indignation (with just the smallest touch of salacious lip-licking?). Religious journals gasped with wonder at the 'courage' of the bishop. What a disgraceful thing — or, alternatively, what a brave thing — that a high officer of the church, charged to shepherd the flock, should venture to say that immorality is wrong and that the ministry has standards!

The second bishop became quite a cult-figure for a while. Stepping sideways from cloistered academic life to the bishop's throne of one of England's greatest cathedrals, he let drop in the media's ears some of his personal doubts and unbeliefs. Doctrines like the virgin birth and the physical resurrection of Christ were not to be taken too seriously. They were images to clothe profound spiritual truths. Shocked reaction in the parishes was followed by a mysterious fire started by a thunderbolt at the Minster, and subsequently (with the bishop still unrepentant) a small earthquake. A cartoon pictured him reading a newspaper placard and asking, 'Was it something I said?'

It all coincided with the visit to England of several of the world's best-known mass evangelists for 'crusades' throughout the country. They preached unashamed supernaturalism in crowded football fields, and something instructive happened. Modern men and women from all walks of life stepped forward in commitment to Jesus Christ. Secular modern man, with all his sophistication, still needs and welcomes the message of the God who intervenes and brings new birth.

The churches were urged to start nurture-groups. Quoting

New Testament, and precedents from every period of spiritual renewal, the evangelists appealed for pastoral care to people in small groups. *There* the Bible could be explained and applied, practical questions answered, pastoral care exercised, spiritual disciplines taught, moral issues sorted out. *There*, converts would become disciples.

I knew perfectly well what would happen — from past experience. Converts would be plunged into a bewildering new world with odd customs, unfamiliar language, and standards of behaviour startlingly different. They would bring problems that would have no easy rule-of-thumb solution, and situations which at first they would not see as problems.

'Can the church help me to find another flat for me and my boyfriend?' asked one such, of an astonished elder. 'I shall have to leave my husband now,' said another to me, 'he forbids everything I go in for — drinking, disco-dancing, C.B. radio, now this — it'll be the last straw.'

There will be shocks and strains for the church, too. For eager new recruits will ask 'Why?' when they meet our funny customs — and sometimes we shan't be able to give credible answers. 'We've always done it this way' may sound comforting to the person who says it, but it will not sound convincing to the person who hears it.

'Oh, but I could never join *this* church,' said one very modern and rather radical student. 'I want to be *baptised*, because the Bible tells me to, but I could never be a *member*.' Why not? The horror on his face was genuine. 'Well, because I could never bring my friends to a place like this!' To us, it was a thriving, successful church. To him it was an excruciatingly middle-class establishment ghetto. In fact, with time and patience, he began to see it differently. His friends came, and some were converted.

Today, *nurture* is rightly emphasised. But can a church offer nurture if its leadership is ambivalent about morals and equivocal about doctrine?

At that stage, a publisher asked me to write a book on church discipline. My first reaction was that of the familiar Western film: tall quiet stranger arrives in lawless frontier town and is offered the sheriff's badge. He is going to stir up trouble and win few friends. I recalled the end of my first pastorate in the north-east of England, where all the problems of these paragraphs had been experienced, intermixed with the fiery Geordie temperament. I told the folk that it was rather like being marshall of Dodge City, but it was worth it. Would *this* be worth it?

Discipline must be one of the most neglected topics of the

modern western church. Indeed, many Christians are unfamiliar with the word or the idea. I used the phrase at a clergy-fraternal once, and the vicar asked, 'Excuse me, what do you mean by church discipline?' A helpful Methodist intervened (with some embarrassment) and explained that it was an approach that used to be applied by Nonconformists.

THE VOICE OF CHRISTIAN HISTORY

In fact it was the third of the three features of a New Testament church, as defined (eventually) by the leaders of the Protestant Reformation. Where the word of God is rightly preached, the sacraments are rightly administered *and discipline is rightly exercised* — there is the church of God, they said. The forefathers of our evangelical free-church Christianity said the same — in fact they taught it to the Reformers. 'Where this is lacking, there is certainly no church, even if Baptism and the Supper of Christ are practised,' wrote Balthasar Hubmaier, perhaps their greatest theologian.

The powerful figure of John Calvin opposed them at first, but finally came to the same conclusion. 'The church without discipline is like a body without sinews,' he said.

The massive mind of John Owen, chaplain to Oliver Cromwell, and theologian *par excellence* of the Puritans, was focused on the subject. He described discipline as:

The due exercise of that authority and power which the Lord Christ has granted for its continuance, increase and preservation in purity, order and holiness according to His appointment.

AND STILL TODAY...

Writers, preachers and thinkers this century have continued to say it. G. Campbell Morgan, twice minister of the great Westminster Chapel in London, commented,

Loss of discipline in today's church weakens the testimony. History shows that the Church pure is the Church powerful; and the Church patronized and tolerant towards evil is the church puerile and paralysed.[1]

J. Oswald Sanders, New Zealand missionary-statesman, wrote,

There is the necessity to maintain godly and living discipline if divine standards are to be maintained, especially in matters of soundness in the faith, morals and Christian conduct.[2]

Mainstream — Baptists for Life and Growth — says in its members' journal,

Church discipline is about the credibility of the Church ... we do well to wrestle with these issues together, so that once again we shall have the right to call ourselves God's holy people.[3]

John Howard Yoder, one of today's most perceptive Christian thinkers, goes so far as to maintain that in the Acts of the Apostles, the gift of the Holy Spirit is more often spoken of in association with discernment, judging, exerting discipline and forgiving after discipline, than in relation to witnessing. He says, 'If practiced, it would change the life of churches more fundamentally than has yet been suggested by the currently popular discussions of changing church structures.'[4]

The House Churches, fastest-growing wing of the charismatic movement in Britain, have a whole system of discipline, shepherding and 'covering' as their most distinctive (and sometimes controversial) feature.

At the annual conference of the Evangelical Free Church of America in 1979, it was resolved,

In the light of declining discipline in godly living in the Body of Christ and the local church, we affirm the responsibility of the local church to give direction and correction to members under its care and to faithfully teach the whole counsel of God.

In the light of the declining appreciation for authority in our society, we call upon the members of our church constituency to be responsive to the care and direction given by the spiritual leadership of the local church.

In the light of God's purpose to purify a people to be holy, we affirm the responsibility of the local church to deal with known sin in its membership in a caring and loving manner.

WHY HAS CHURCH DISCIPLINE BEEN ABANDONED?

There are many reasons. Some of them are discreditable, and some understandable. As always, misuse has led to disuse, and exaggeration to abandonment.

Dogmatic Christianity is out of favour. The rot set in during Victorian times, grew as scholars questioned the authority of the Bible, and became complete in our own day of anti-authoritarianism. Dogmatic clarity about anything is regarded with suspicion. The open mind, the tolerant stance, the give-and-take attitude; these are today's virtues. If people no longer believe that God has actually spoken in clear unequivocal words that have a definable meaning, then they will hesitate to condemn outright any belief as wrong, and any behaviour as bad. A lady said naively to me — 'I would like to join your Free Church, so that I shall be free to believe anything I like.' I quickly disillusioned her, but her expectation would be reasonable in some congregations.

Permissiveness has won the day. The wholesale abandonment of moral standards in the last forty years has made ethical discussion almost meaningless. Moreover, the church is filling with new converts who are already locked in moral dilemmas from which there is no apparent way of escape. The modern church leader is not unlike a Victorian missionary to Africa facing polygamy, witchcraft and slavery as an integral part of society. How can he draw lines when they have all been crossed already?

Sectarianism is rampant. There is little sense of the church as one body, holding amongst its varied branches one faith and one morality. If a member dislikes the stance of one church, he can leave and join another, where as likely as not he will be eagerly welcomed. If his desire to speak in tongues is regulated in one church, he can find another more charismatic. If one vicar will not remarry him, another can be found who will. If his homosexuality is condemned in biblical terms in one church, he can travel to another made up of gay Christians. In view of this, is enforcing discipline worth the trouble?

Rigid rules are out of date. This is not surprising. In the comparatively simple world before Hitler's war, an evangelical knew where he stood. As evidence of conversion, he was expected to give up drinking, dancing and cinema attendance. This expectation reflected a particular social milieu which has passed away. We see now that 'worldliness' is a lot more subtle than attendance at certain buildings, and that spirituality is a lot more complex than assent to some simple bans. Every few years rapid change brings problems with apparent worldliness. In two of my three pastorates I had to battle against the assertion of older members that a converted teenage girl could not wear a leather jacket and knee-length hair, whilst jeans and collar-length hair on a youth cast serious doubts on his conversion. There was not one remote scriptural argument for this, of course; the unspoken and unconscious assumption was that converts become middle-aged and middle-class overnight. The enlistment of real people from the real world into its ranks (by conversion) has faced the church with a multitude of problems, ills, dilemmas, challenges and relationships which simply cannot be resolved by the quoting of a rule. Life is not like that, and the New Testament is not written like that. This humbling discovery has now led to an over-reaction, in which the church hesitates to have any rules at all.

The church has lost its nerve.   Many local congregations have scarcely seen a genuine conversion from 'outside' in a member's life-time. Family continuance and transfer from another area have accounted for much apparent church growth. Where social conditions make these factors unlikely, the church simply dies out. When recruits are rare, no one wishes to reduce their number even further by making life difficult for them. I knew a famous open-air preacher who went out so far to meet and accommodate his unbelieving audience that finally there was little to distinguish him from them. But the result was not lots of conversions; he has publicly written that he never saw one. You will not persuade someone to sell his bicycle and buy a motorcar by strongly emphasising that, since both have wheels and run along roads, there is little to choose between them. If there is little choice, he will not choose. Efforts to make the Christian community almost indistinguishable from its environment have proved disastrous. No one has bothered to join us. A ministerial friend told me sadly how he had gone through a spell when he followed this course. He got totally involved in the 'servant-church role,' occupying himself with problems of housing and welfare, bringing his influence onto the borough council, and eventually becoming mayor. Many people were grateful to him … 'and not a single one joined my church,' he told me, when he returned to preaching the gospel. Then they did.

A false note has been sounded in the past. There is no doubt about this. Some church discipline went too far. The presbytery as an inquisition, the church meeting like a Star Chamber, the vicar a benevolent dictator (and not always benevolent), the parochial church council a hot-bed of social snobbery; all of these have been factors in robbing discipline of its true meaning. People know, or think they know, about past practices through television soap operas and colourful historical romances. They know about the witch trials of Salem, the pregnant servant girls put out on the street, the penitent-stool, the chapel deacon who punishes drunkenness in the choir but submits his men to gross injustice at the mill. They know about missionaries who act like colonial administrators, or make the natives destroy their beautiful and natural customs. Sometimes fact, and sometimes caricature, it is enough to put a question mark over the whole subject. Discipline is seen as condemnation and punishment, rather than support, encouragement, guidance and protection — with restoration and forgiveness where necessary.

Nobody feels good enough. What right have I to judge my brother? That is a sensitive question often sincerely asked. Who am I to say he is wrong? I am a sinner myself. I don't know all the details, so it would be unfair to criticise. Is not *love* the better way? Would it not be more compassionate to leave things as they are?

Church structure can be unworkable. Religious subjectivism has invaded whole denominations so that some lack the will and others lack the means to exert discipline.

The search for truth is now lauded as the church's greatest activity — an odd attitude in view of the Bible's constant assertion that the truth has already been 'committed to us' (Jude 3) and is to be declared by us. Whether love for the God of truth might perhaps include love for the truth of God is apparently still a matter for debate.

Other groups also set understandable value on freedom. Baptists, for example, pioneered religious and civil liberty in the western world. They presented the first arguments in the English language for liberty of conscience. Their case was a biblical one. The only conviction worth anything is a freely reached conviction. The only persuasion allowable in New Testament terms is moral and spiritual persuasion. The only being with the ability and authority to dictate to a man's conscience is the God he worships. All true; and early Baptists and other Separatists paid dearly for it, to the gain of the whole world. But that has become misunderstood and misapplied. Baptists sometimes glory in their freedom from creeds and statements of faith. They have never valued or heeded such things, it is said, for truth is too big to be defined in words. This is a factual error. The Baptist forefathers often used carefully detailed creeds, catechisms and confessions of faith. What they denied was the value of *enforcing* such creeds.

When a college principal a few years ago used expressions which at the very least raised questions about his commitment to the deity of Christ, it was said at first that nothing could or should be done about it. We should rejoice in freedom of interpretation. The college in question was independent. Creeds could not be imposed. Witch hunts were to be deplored. In the event, the great mass of Baptists proved to be sound at heart. Firm commitment to the doctrine of the Trinity was expressed at a general assembly. The implications were left for each church and college to work out for itself. But at least they had escaped from the snare of a sincere but muddled 'liberty' which would have cast doubts on commitment to revealed truth. It was a narrow squeak. The heart-searching involved in it made many Baptists think hard about where they were going, and proved to be one of several features which led to a 'new look' and a surge of healthy life in the denomination. But it did raise serious questions about the ability of the 'independent' system to exercise meaningful discipline.

THE PROBLEMS OF DEFINITION

The above story had a curious epilogue. The controversy proved the last straw for numbers of churches, who abandoned the Baptist Union. Shortly afterwards several of them met to organise a new affiliation or union. In the light of the recent problems, they agreed to have a detailed statement of faith ... and then found they could not agree on one. The breaking point was the problem of the fate of the impenitent unbeliever after death. Some believed in an eternal conscious hell, some believed in immediate loss and destruction, some were not happy with a test of faith on the subject. The hope of an affiliation was abandoned. Now what are the comparative values of the doctrine of the Trinity and the details of what it means to be 'lost'? What is fundamental, the irreducible minimum of sound doctrine, so to speak?

It is a problem for morality as well as behaviour. Is discipline only possible if, for example, the church has an exactly defined stance on marriage, divorce and remarriage? Would there be any hope of reaching agreement? The New Testament teaching may at first seem clear. What terminates a marriage? Only the immorality of one of the partners (Matthew 5:32). But just a moment, what about desertion (1 Corinthians 7:15)? Already the issue is becoming complicated by an apostolic permission.

This used to be almost a hypothetical argument and no more. Only when the practical question arose halfway through my second pastorate did I discover how equally dedicated Christians can come to very different conclusions. To my great surprise I found that people who agree with my understanding that immorality may terminate a marriage, do not follow that with the (to me) obvious corollary that remarriage of the 'innocent partner' in such a case is permissible. Even more surprising, I discovered Christians who did not see divorce and remarriage as a problem at all. Problems of definition, then, cause some to despair of ever maintaining discipline.

THE TRIUMPH OF INDIVIDUALISM

This is more marked in America, but is evident in Europe too. Endless talk of 'human rights,' 'liberty of conscience,' 'the integrity of the individual,' etc. (all proper in its place) has undermined Christian community life when taken out of context.

When a Church of Christ congregation expelled a member for having a long-term affair with a local public figure, she filed a lawsuit against the elders and members for 'inflicting emotional distress and invading privacy.' The church had acted in obedience to Christ's words in Matthew 18:15–17 as they understood them. The lady in question declined their private admonition, offered her resignation, and claimed that they could thus no longer 'tell it to the church' as it was 'no longer their business.' The church continued on its course, and was subsequently hit for almost half a million dollars in fines and damages.[5] The lady's testimony in court claimed, 'What I do or do not do is between God and myself,' and that elders had no right to 'mess with someone else's life.'

Her attorney, using less restrained language, suggested that, 'It doesn't matter if she was fornicating up and down the street. It doesn't give [the church] the right to stick their nose in it,' and in his closing speech claimed for his client, 'the right to lead her life the way she chooses.'

This is only one example of a trend in America. The mail that such cases engender from other church members makes sombre reading.

'I cannot believe that church officials would anoint themselves and pass judgement on one of their members.'

'Those who slander and belittle a person in front of a congregation should themselves be disciplined.'

'How a Christian lives his private life is between that person and God, not the elders of the church.'

All of this, as we shall see, makes nonsense of the clear teaching of Christ and his apostles. The fact that it can be said, apparently with sincerity, shows how completely an individualistic approach has swamped the church and made its corporate life practically meaningless. The same country sees 'drive-in churches' (where the family do not leave their car, but plug in for the sermon) and great numbers preferring to watch a televised service rather than actually attending.

CASUALTIES OF THE PERMISSIVE AGE

Of course there are enormous difficulties. We have done without discipline so long that many of our people do not know what it is, and as leaders we will shrink from showing them. We shall run into family problems. How can the eldership discuss this erring member when his father-in-law is a deacon? There will be administrative difficulties. Who makes the decision and takes the action? Is our church structured for it? There will be sensitive issues of confidentiality and trust. There will be painful problems where we may not all agree on our interpretation of Scripture. Let me give two examples.

A middle-aged couple, with their three teenage children, were all attending my baptism-and-membership class after conversion. At the end of the course, the baptism arranged, the parents asked for a private word with me.

'You see, it's like this; we have never been married,' the man told me. 'I have a wife in America who is living with another man and they have two grown children. My wife — well, I mean Jean here, has a husband living with a girl and they have a son. Our children are really *ours*, but they think we are married. How can we admit we are not, at their sensitive age? And we can't marry without getting divorced first, and *that* will let the cat out of the bag. Well, is it really all right for us to join the church?'

What was the answer? 'No, certainly not, for you are living in adultery'? Technically they were. But how could they put matters right? By separating and destroying the family? By becoming the 'guilty parties' in a divorce? By going back to their other partners (thus destroying *three* families — except of course that the other partners would not go along with it). And how could I keep them out of the membership of the local church when Christ has, by grace, made them members of his universal church? Is the church more particular than God? We were a Baptist church, so governed (under God) by the church meeting. Should I then take this to the church meeting — and expose five new converts to embarrassment, gossip and scandal?

I did what seemed right, and must now risk the wrath of book reviewers. I shared it in confidence with one deacon. We agreed that the cross draws a line at conversion. Anything on the 'past' side of that line is forgiven. If restoration or repair is possible it should be offered. If it is not possible, then this side of the line there is a new beginning. The gospel meets people where they are, not where they should be. We agreed to baptise the five, and gave a report to the church meeting on their present commitment to Christ — no mention of the past. Was I right?

A youth leader in the north of England, one of my own sons in the faith, had a very difficult marriage. I cannot share the intimate details, but in his position I cannot imagine how I could have borne it. After years of doing what I would find unimaginably hard, he gave way. A romance began with a colleague in the office. Husband and wife agreed to divorce. He did not share it with any of us, and I had to tackle him about it. The amazing blanking of the mind, which one sees in someone inextricably entangled, was evident. No, he did not feel that the relationship could be cooled at least until there was a divorce. No, he did not feel that divorce need be examined in the light of Scripture. He believed in a loving God, not a judgemental God. Yes, he would certainly resign from office in the church, but not from membership.

Elders were horribly embarrassed and incredulous. They felt *I* should really handle it (a feeling elders can be prone to, I find!). I asked my friend to let me have his resignation from membership of the church without giving a detailed reason ('domestic problems that compromise my witness,' I suggested), otherwise I would have to call for his excommunication at the meeting, and necessarily give details. He agreed, sadly. There were many tears at the church meeting. Restoration to God, though not to this church, is clearly taking place. Did I handle it like a coward, a blackmailer, a dictator, or a faithful pastor? I have my doubts. I have lost one of the finest men I know.

NO OTHER OPTION

These are the problems which church discipline raises — a small sample. Tears and nervous strain and sleepless nights are involved. Everything does not turn out to be discernibly black and white. It is easier to let church discipline stay buried, where most of the western church has left it. But we dare not do that. It must be recovered. It is the muscle and sinew of the church, without which there is no body, but a jellyfish. The church has no chance of presenting a credible witness to the watching world without it. And let there be no doubt — the world is watching. In Britain it is watching as it has never watched before in my lifetime, and I began to preach at the age of fifteen, thirty-eight years ago.

The church is supposed to be a light in the darkness, a city set on a hill. In other words, we are meant to be looked at. The church is supposed to be the 'pillar and ground of the truth.' That is, we should expect to be listened to. We are the people of God, distinguished from a godless world. That means we have to be discernibly different. When church discipline was applied (by God, notice!) in a particularly drastic manner to a situation where testimony was being denied, people queued up to join, or fell over each other to get away.

> Nobody outside dared to join them, even though the people spoke highly of them. But more and more people were added to the group — a crowd of men and women who believed in the Lord.
>
> Acts 5:14, cf verses 1–11

A credible church must be a disciplined church. How is it done?

Notes

1.   G. Campbell Morgan, *Commentary on First Corinthians*, London, Oliphants, 1947.
2.   J. Oswald Sanders, in *Today* (June 1984).
3.   In *Mainstream*, 15 (January 1984).
4.   John Howard Yoder, in *Concern*, 14 (February 1967).
5.   Lynn Buzzard, 'Is church discipline an invasion of privacy?' in *Christianity Today* (9 November 1984).

CHAPTER TWO

The Master and his Men

GALILEE is a beautiful place. As you drop down over the hills from Nazareth, the lake lies before you, a pool of placid blue garrisoned by rolling mountains. Sometimes the colour changes to a sullen pewter, ruffled by chill winds that funnel down the valleys and tear the waves into fury in a matter of moments. On the gentler slopes of the northern shore is the 'Evangelical Triangle' of Capernaum, Chorazin and Bethsaida, where 'most of his mighty works were done.' Christ's solemn warning has been fulfilled (Matthew 11:20–24) and they all lie in ruins now, whilst, ironically, the pagan Tiberius, never mentioned in the gospel story and frowned on by contemporary Jews for its Roman ways, still flourishes as a kind of modern Israeli Brighton.

This was no rural backwater in the time of Jesus. Major imperial trade-routes and military roads traversed the province. Capernaum was on a T-junction, and flourished as the centre for commerce and taxation, with a world-wide fish exporting trade.

A fact that startles the traveller today is the small scale of it all. Row half a mile off shore, and one camera shot will encapsulate most of the well-known events of the Gospel narratives. But, strangely, the opposite is also true. To the east is Decapolis, with the ten pagan cities that gave it its name. To the north, Syro-Phoenicia. Here, in Jordan, Lebanon and Syria as they are today, Jesus took great sweeping mission-journeys far outside Jewry. They must have been stupendous walks.

Events were mounting to a climax for the disciples. Immense vistas impossible for them yet to comprehend were opening up before them. They were into something vastly more than the fellowship of learners following a rabbi. The world-wide church was being formed. But first, the crucifixion and resurrection.

This climax came on the last of Jesus' great journey. He gathered his disciples together at pagan Caesarea Philippi (now called Banyas) to sum up what they had learned about him, and what conclusions they had come to (Matthew 16:13–20). From there they returned to their home-province. Then, one more earnest, urgent talk with them, and Galilee would be left behind (Matthew 19:1). The disciples were about to become apostles. Matthew 18 gives us the substance of that last talk. It is an apostolic commission to church-building, government and discipline. (This, at any rate, is how Matthew presents the facts from his characteristic point of view.)

One of the strangest ironies of Christian history is the church's misuse of the word *apostle*. It has come to connote princely power, crushing authority, absolutism in religion. We get mental images of purple robes and kingly splendour, of bishops who make medieval kings kneel in the snow, or 'apostolic delegates' who make emperors tremble. It is very different from the New Testament reality. Peter and Paul delighted to describe themselves as slaves — servants of people because servants of God. The 'signs of an apostle' of which they spoke were not only the stunning effect of 'signs and wonders' but a whole life of service, self-giving, suffering, derision, rejection (II Corinthians 11).

At the beginning they had their illusions, of course. This last great 'discourse' in which Jesus coached them for leadership sprang from one of these illusions. Having just been doubly warned of the coming cross (Matthew 16:21, and 17:9), Jesus' band of followers had promptly forgotten what they could not emotionally accept (Matthew 16:22–23). While Jesus mused sadly on coming shame and suffering, they indulged in gleeful dreams of promotion in the Kingdom (Matthew 18:1). Worse still, it is fatally easy to move from the thought, 'I shall be great,' to the thought '...greater than my brother, I hope.'

The last journey to Jerusalem was near. In what has been called 'the last Galilean task,' Jesus was anxious to press on his men the principles on which their community would work when he had gone. Church discipline, in fact, was the subject in his mind. How will the church function as the people of Christ's presence, preserving purity, powerful in prayer, engaged in a work that touches earth with the awesome authority of heaven? This is the question answered in his long talk with them. *Discipline can only be exercised by the disciplined* — in fact by disciples.

A CHILD IN THE MIDST

So — master communicator that he is, he gives an object lesson that will never be forgotten (though we still manage either to misunderstand it or to reduce it to sentimentalism). 'He called a child, made him stand in front of them, and said, "I assure you that unless you change and become like children, you will never enter the kingdom of heaven" (Matthew 18:2–3).

What is it about a child that paves the pathway to Christian leadership? *The ability to trust* is often suggested. There is truth in that, but not here. The word 'converted' (AV) coupled with the idea of new birth (becoming a child) leads others to make the need for *evangelical conversion* the main thrust. Certainly the attitude looked for will only come through new birth, but again that is not the main point. (It is a melancholy fact that crisis-conversion does *not* automatically lead to a humble spirit. The proposition, 'evangelicals are the humblest of mankind' will not survive much examination.) The context declares the meaning. *Unpretentiousness* is the child-attitude which comes so easily to infants and so hard to adults. They embarrass parents by showing no need to impress others until they are carefully shown differently. Now what children are unconsciously, *without* being taught, adults must become consciously *by* being taught. That, says Jesus, is the pathway to promotion in his kingdom and his church.

THE WAY UP IS DOWN

This is not self-deprecation — that shift of the embarrassed, the mock-humble and the evader of responsibility (as well as, sometimes, the emotionally hurt). Not self-deprecation but self-oblivion, is what Jesus teaches; the attitude of the man too involved in self-giving service to have time, energy or inclination for self-defence and self-aggrandisement.

We all know people like that. I recall Sister Winifred of Gateshead. In the grim streets of English Tyneside, through the poverty, slump and squalor of the 1920's and 1930's, she moved amongst people who scraped an existence in slums, who even slept in empty barrels on the street or under upturned barrows. Tiny and delicate, with a tubercular spine and a sparrow-like chirpiness, she gave up what was vaguely referred to as a 'lady's life' and founded 'The Vineyard' (Vine Street Mission). Social welfare, soup-kitchens, rescue of 'fallen girls,' robust gospel-preaching indoors and out, occupied every waking hour. When a publican demanded a kiss from her because he had a collecting-box in his pub, she vowed never again to ask for money 'from the world.' When the local police gave her a bodyguard she shooed them away, depending only on the Lord (they put men in plainclothes after that, and she never knew). I worked briefly with her in the 1960's, and she died still in leadership in the 1970's, her Mission membership listing very large numbers of men who accepted her sometimes peremptory leadership because she was totally committed to self-giving.

People like that are the 'great' in Christ's kingdom. Notice, there is no false equality. Jesus does not answer the question, 'Who is the greatest?' with 'No one, for all are equal.' Rather, he replies, 'Not you, because you asked. You display the spirit that leads to demotion, not promotion.' But the promotion is available. He who dares, may have it, without looking for it. Indeed, he who is looking for it is unqualified to get it. All this is in line with that famous dictum of Mark's Gospel, the basic principle of Christian leadership.

> You know that the men who are considered rulers of the heathen have power over them.... This, however, is not the way it is among you. If one of you wants to be great, he must be the servant of the rest; and if one of you wants to be first, he must be the slave of all. For even the Son of Man did not come to be served; he came to serve.
>
> Mark 10:42–45

There, succinctly, is the difference between God's kingdom and human sovereignty. The difference lies in the principle on which promotion proceeds. Interestingly, Mark sets that saying in the context of another quarrel amongst the disciples about 'jobs for the boys' in the kingdom (verses 35–41).

VULNERABLE PEOPLE

In a typical rabbinical way Jesus then jumped from the thought of being like children to the concept of *handling childlike people*. The picture of *leaders* childlike in their humility switches to a picture of *those who are led*, childlike in their vulnerability. How true this is. I sometimes marvel at the ease with which followers can be led. They pour through the Garden Tomb where I minister in Jerusalem, each with their pastor, or their group leader, or their professional guide. Some will march stolidly after their appointed head, looking where he points, listening when he speaks, moving where he directs, startled and embarrassed if someone questions or checks him. Others will accept anything and everything from someone who is sufficiently dynamic and extrovert. I have heard sheer absurdities swallowed whole without so much as a cough. The temptation to mislead the gullible and mould the malleable seems to be irresistible to some leaders. Let them beware. They are handling plastic material, but there is such a thing as plastic explosive, and it can blow up in your hands. We shall give account to God for what we do in the way of moulding, and how we do it. The horrifying suicides of Jonestown, the mesmerism of the Moonies' mass-weddings, warn us against misuse.

> If anyone should cause one of these little ones to lose his faith in me, it would be better for that person to have a large millstone tied round his neck and be drowned in the deep sea.... Such things will always happen — but how terrible for the one who causes them!
>
> Matthew 18:6–7

Some itinerants in the charismatic road-show could afford to ponder that one.

A leadership gift that sways people, a counselling gift that draws people, a healing gift that brings the weak, the worried, the sick and the sad to your vestry door or your correspondence column; these may well be gifts from God, but misused they become millstones indeed, to exploiter and exploited. Some of us should be looking very hard at our stock answers which were once built on genuine proven experience but have now become glib techniques that give us power over people. A close look would be healthy, too, at those glossy trans-Atlantic TV shows in which the well-groomed, gleaming-toothed, fast-talking preacher spills out his faith-promoting anodynes and offers promotion, a new car, a bigger bank balance or simply peace of mind for the worried and lonely—to those who keep covenant with God and send the dollars to his twenty-two-inch-screen servant.

STERN SELF-DISCIPLINE

I knew a humble open-air evangelist who was a wizard with visual aids. He produced them with card and paint, with imaginative flair and with a lot of hard work. Every couple of years he destroyed them all and started on new ones. It broke my heart to see them go. But my friend found that before long he was depending on his artistic skill and his ingenious slogans to sway people. So he destroyed the lot, and went back to prayer and fasting. He never got as far as exploiting people, but the danger was

17

there, and he cut it off.

That was Christ's command: 'If your hand or your foot makes you lose your faith, cut it off and throw it away!' (Matthew 18:8).

SOMEONE IS WATCHING

Still more strongly come words of warning and challenge to those who influence people and sway their lives. Contempt can creep into our attitudes so easily. Staff meetings of my church pastoral team, I have always found, were great places for humour. We worked off our frustrations over demanding people, complaining members, crabby characters, with a little playful humour (and just a trace of exaggeration, perhaps). It was good and healthy. A comparison of some tough trouble-making lady in the choir with Bertie Wooster's Aunt Agatha (who ate broken bottles and six-inch nails for breakfast, you remember) has lightened a load, removed the sting of bitterness, and helped us to see things in perspective. But it can go too far, and with fatal ease turn to contempt.

'See that you don't despise any of these little ones. Their angels in heaven, I tell you, are always in the presence of my Father in heaven' (Matthew 18:10). Thus, in a breath-taking glimpse, Jesus shows his apostles that very celestial kingdom in which they so much wanted to be prominent. Look there! Glorious angels around the throne are deeply concerned about the welfare of God's little ones. And look again! The Son of God leaves heaven and, like a shepherd seeking the one lost sheep, searches for those who have gone astray, not shutting them out of the fold but going to any lengths to bring them back in (verses 12–14). That is leadership. There is shepherding.

Only now does Jesus approach the subject of active church discipline. It is to be exercised by people who show this kind of attitude — a far cry from the hard-faced, purse-lipped legalistic way in which it has sometimes been practised. Here are the basic principles. We must preserve the purity of our relationships in the Fellowship (18:15–16). We must reluctantly dismiss those who persistently offend and refuse to mend their ways (18:17). We may exercise the awesome power to 'bind and loose,' for we are handling spiritual things (18:18–19). We must be ready to forgive, and eager to restore, careful to avoid personal vindictiveness (18:21–35). That is church discipline in embryo. Here, already expounded in Galilee, are all the elements of Paul's discipline at Corinth.

RELATIONS IN TURMOIL (18:15–16)

'If your brother sins against you, go to him and show him his fault.' The Gospel is all about relationships, vertical and horizontal. A Christian denies these relationships by his personal injury, anger, jealousy, gossip, verbal abuse, injustice, quarrelling, or whatever. This is the sin of Corinth, shown in sexual misbehaviour on the one hand and selfishness at the Lord's Table on the other. For *this* 'some slept,' as we shall see.

I recall a church-membership instruction class. All of the members were housewives, newly converted. I had explained how a Baptist church works: its self-governing church meetings, its 'right hand of fellowship' extended to the new members on behalf of all, its partnership with the pastor. One lady saw the implications in a flash, and was so startled that she interrupted me. 'But that means that *I* make the church what it is! I find that scaring!' A few months later, this same group, now a house-cell within the church, ran into a nasty little crisis. 'Sharing' turned to gossip, the fault of one had scandalised another, and the lady who had interrupted me was upset, offended and talking of 'leaving.' I gently reminded her of her own reaction a little time ago. 'It *is* scaring, but you took it on,' I said. 'Now when you hit your first problem you have to see it through.' She took the point, accepted the gentle rebuke, and before long had seen her husband and teenage sons converted and in the fellowship.

But notice how tactfully and sensitively the issue must be tackled. See Matthew 18:15–16: 'Do it privately,' just between yourselves. 'If he will not listen to you, take one or two other persons with you.' The privacy gives every incentive to make adjustments with the minimum of embarrassment. It tests the motive of the offended party. It gives him no room for gossip or scandal, and puts a bridle on his lips. It offers no leeway to officious busybodies to spread the trouble. The 'witnesses,' when they are necessary, discourage either party from excessive reactions or later trouble-making accusations.

EXCLUDED FROM THE FELLOWSHIP (18:17)

'If he will not listen to them, then tell the whole thing to the church. Finally, if he will not listen to the church, treat him as though he was a pagan or a tax-collector.'

The solemnity of this is underlined by the fact that this is one of only two recorded references to 'church' made by Jesus. (However, the word would be no puzzle to his hearers, who were accustomed to hearing Israel in its religious aspect — the people of God — described as *ecclesia* in their Greek Old Testament).

What does verse 17 mean? The Christian who wilfully continues on a course which is destroying or denying the fellowship, may have to be excluded from it. That means no *religious* contact at all, and as little *social* contact as is strictly necessary. 'Pagans,' by definition, had no place in the worship of God. 'Tax collectors' were social pariahs, for they worked for the godless enemy and exploited the people of Israel.

Are we, then, to treat the offender with hostility and hatred? Not at all. Jesus is using 'pagan' and 'tax-collectors' metaphorically. In any case, remember that he was 'the friend of tax-collectors and sinners'! But a solemn statement from the church that a member is seriously out of step and must be excluded will, in fact, have the effect that Jesus suggests. He will stop worshipping with the church and will slip into other interests, pursuits and friendships. Break the religious tie and he will break the social tie! The instruction also makes it impossible for the offender to defy church leaders, creep around to other members for their sympathy and support, and cause further division.

Here is a delicate subject indeed. Before arguing that the churches have failed to deal effectively with church discipline, we must be clear about what we mean by 'effective.' Situations change: church discipline is never absolute, either in the New Testament or today. It is *conditional* (for it is dependent on attitudes), it is *therapeutic* (for it is designed to lead to restoration) and it is *adjustable* (because of the variety of problems that it must tackle). Nevertheless, *it expresses absolutes*, for God has not left us to work out our own standards.

Here is great tension. That tension only has some chance of being resolved if church discipline is seen not as the passing of a *sentence* (only God can do that) but as the confronting of a *problem* and the application of a remedy.

Of course 'excommunication' (let us now call it that) is a sad and terrible thing. That is why Jesus commands careful, prayerful, private pleading in the hope of averting it. But his love for each follower of his (expressed in those very commands) must be balanced by his love for his whole church. So must ours. The law of love is the basis for church discipline: love for each member, and love for the whole. Precisely because I am bound by love to welcome every member as my brother and sister, so I am bound to be concerned about every member's behaviour.

20

CHAPTER THREE

The Mandate for the Church

MATTHEW 18 is dynamite. We have to go a lot further yet in exploring its meaning. Over and over again we shall see it appealed to by almost every significant movement of reformation and renewal in church history. The brave Waldensians in dark medieval days of persecution appealed to it. The underground Moravian Brethren astonished the Protestant Reformers by their application of it. The gallant Anabaptist Movement which was virtually quenched in its own blood had it as its rallying-cry and *raison d'être*. John Calvin's much maligned experiment in Geneva drew inspiration from it. The revived Moravians of Wesley's day took it as their foundation and won Wesley for Christ. He in turn adapted it for the use of the best-organised revival movement that the English world has ever known. The twentieth-century East African Revival is based on its teaching.

A modern-day writer, often proved truly prophetic, draws our attention to it in forthright terms:

> It gives more authority to the church than does Rome, trusts more to the Holy Spirit than does Pentecostalism, has more respect for the individual than Humanism, makes more moral standards than Puritanism, is more open to the given situation than the 'New Morality.'[1]

It is time to continue our exploration.

PROHIBITING AND PERMITTING (18:18–19)

> And so I tell all of you: what you prohibit on earth will be prohibited in heaven, and what you permit on earth will be permitted in heaven.

We suddenly seem to be in a different dimension. 'Binding' and 'loosing' are words used in the Authorised Version, and most modern translations attempt an interpretation as much as a translation. What does it mean? The rabbis of Jesus' day used the phrase. The whole style of rabbinical teaching for the Jews consisted of sayings, anecdotes, and appeals to precedent. Problems were brought to them and cases submitted for their advice and judgement. Suppose a man's house set on fire on the Sabbath. Could he 'work' by rescuing his furniture and belongings from the blaze? Scriptures were consulted, other examples referred to, opinions taken, and an answer given: carrying what you are wearing does not count as work, so you may rescue anything you wear. That raises another question: could you take your coat off outside, run back in, put another on, and rescue that in turn? And what about, perhaps, wearing a table or a portable bed? And so the discussion would go on, and the judgements be made.

Now this whole process was called binding and loosing. '*This* principle, and *this* example, and *this* anecdote apply to your situation' — that was 'binding' (Hebrew: *assar,* he bound). 'This one does not' — that was 'loosing' (Hebrew: *hittir,* he permitted). The whole process was channelled in two different directions. It could be *legislative.* That is, certain rules and regulations and definitions were agreed on and made 'law.' It could be *judicial.* That is, someone could be brought before a court charged with an offence. By examining the behaviour and the precendents, the rabbis would declare him guilty or innocent.

This enormous mass of verbal material was eventually gathered together (in the fourth century AD) as the *Talmud.* Corporately it was (and is) referred to as *Halakah.* This almost untranslatable Hebrew word (used as it stands in modern English in Israel today) means something like '*the way to walk*.' Halakah is still a very live issue. A Jerusalem newspaper will often contain lively discussion about it. Anyone wishing to become a Jew (to embrace Judaism) must do it 'according to Halakah,' under the instruction of a totally fundamentalist orthodox teacher (to the indignation of liberal and conservative and reformed rabbis!). It causes very great problems to someone already a Jew, who wishes to become a Christian.

The rabbis of Jesus' day took this immensely seriously. They suggested that heaven actually has a celestial Sanhedrin, so to speak. The Sanhedrin Above confirms what the Sanhedrin Below has decided, they claimed. After all, is it not all drawn from the Law of God?

WHAT DID JESUS MEAN?

Can Jesus possibly have meant that his church would be bound by a similar mass of precedent and regulation? A canon law, in fact, with apostles administering it like a Christian Sanhedrin? In some features of material and style, the Sermon on the mount resembles rabbinical legislation. Yet there is a vast difference which Jesus' hearers immediately sensed. 'He taught with authority, not like the teachers of the law,' they said in amazement (Matthew 7:28–29). He did *not* balance opinion with comment and precedent. He said, 'This is what God wants' and 'I say to you' — the direct authority of God. Moreover, he had little time for the mass of tradition. Quoting one piece of Halakah, he storms, 'In this way you disregard God's command, in order to follow your own teaching' — and quotes Isaiah's words, 'They teach man-made rules as though they were my [God's] laws' (Matthew 15:3–9).

What did Jesus mean by the church's binding and loosing, then? There are several possibilities. The Jewish Christian writer Albert Edersheim sees it as contrast. The pharisees made *pretensions* to their great authority, but Jesus is saying in effect — 'No, they get it all wrong. But in my church, simple fishermen and tax-collectors will get it right, because my Spirit is with them.'

Or perhaps he is using the words purely as illustration to show that there is some analogy with the vast, detailed, all-pervasive system of the pharisees, because the divine authority they hope for is in fact given to the gathered church … and in the ongoing experience of its members, the precedents and applications will be hammered out.

Or perhaps, again, Jesus is using familiar and evocative words to describe that remarkable authority present in the church. Once only exalted teachers could claim it; now every humble disciple, taking his proper place in the activity of the church, can know something of it.

'This mandate makes the church the church,' says Yoder.

But the question still remains — is Jesus talking simply about forgiveness, or about all church decisions?

THE CHURCH — WHERE IT HAPPENS

Certainly it is significant that the only two recorded occasions when Jesus spoke of 'the church' are both associated with binding and loosing.

Simon Peter answered, 'You are the Messiah, the Son of the living God.'

[Jesus said] '... on this rock foundation I will build my church.... I will give you the keys of the Kingdom of heaven; what you prohibit on earth will be prohibited in heaven, and what you permit on earth will be permitted in heaven.'

Matthew 16:16–19

The meaning is clear, replies Jesus. Peter (on behalf of the disciples) has made that confession of confidence in Christ which constitutes saving faith and entry into the church. It will go on happening. Peter (and the others) will propagate that same faith — in other words, will preach the gospel. Doing so, they will be able to state with authority and certainty that those who believe will be saved, and those who reject will perish — thus employing 'the keys' which were synonymous with 'binding and loosing.' In point of fact, Peter himself first used the keys with Jews on the day of Pentecost in Jerusalem, and with non-Jews on the 'Gentile Pentecost' at Caesarea (Acts 2 and Acts 10).

Jesus' later promise at Easter was to *all* of the disciples, and was associated with the gift of the Holy Spirit.

As the Father sent me, so I send you.... Receive the Holy Spirit. If you forgive people's sins, they are forgiven; if you do not forgive them, they are not forgiven.

John 20:19–23

Jesus so closely relates his gospel to his church that faithful preachers of that gospel and members of that church are spoken of as if they do the forgiving! God in heaven confirms by his Spirit the faithful word and witness of Christ's people on earth: they announce pardon on God's terms, and God gives his Spirit to those who accept.

That seems to bring Matthew 18 back to forgiveness, rather than church legislation. After all, that was the point of the private rebuke and the interview before witnesses of the early verses (15–16). It was the point of the parable of the lost sheep (10–14). It will yet be the point of Peter's question and the parable of the unmerciful servant (21–35). What could be clearer than the final words?

And Jesus concluded, That is how my Father in heaven will treat every one of you unless you forgive your brother from your heart.

Matthew 18:35

FORGIVENESS — THE GOSPEL IN ACTION

That simple reflection should be enough to save harsh church discipline from majoring on punishment rather than pardon, as it so often has. The whole purpose is to remove the offence by gently pointing it out — privately if possible. If it becomes a matter of public discipline, it is still in the hope of restoration. Hence Peter's question, so naively put: 'How many times do I have to forgive him? Seven times?' (verse 21). The rabbis suggested six, so Peter no doubt felt he was making a handsome offer. 'Seventy times seven' becomes uncountable, of course. Only someone gripped in the bonds of vindictiveness is going to be able to remember four hundred and ninety pardons and then refuse the next one. So the 'binding and loosing' refers most obviously to this forgiving process. It is the reconciled community displaying and illustrating the gospel by its internal attitudes. For what sense or power is there in proclaiming to an unbelieving world that God has reconciled us to himself, if before their very eyes we are failing to be reconciled to each other?

A Christian lady in the Midlands, convicted by a sermon, confessed to me her involvement in a serious offence against her employer. Repentance was real, restitution was fully made, and the magistrates acknowledged that this offence would never have been discovered had she not admitted it. Pressure was put on me to withhold forgiveness and restoration to church membership, especially as she was a personal friend. 'It will look like favouritism,' I was warned. The eldership stood with me, as I stood with her in the trial. The whole court case was a public witness to the gospel. A watching community had the gospel preached to it, and admitted as much. Instead of the evangelistic witness being hindered (as it might well have been) there was no diminution in the regular trickle of conversions. 'God is a God of new beginnings,' I had written to my friend when it happened.

Sadly, the church often finds it hard to forgive, not only genuine sins for which Christ died, but 'offences' which are imaginary. Social stigma, class distinction, the generation gap, styles of clothing and hair and language — all of these often set Christian against Christian. A church that is seeing people added by conversion in any significant numbers must learn to 'forgive' the wearing of jeans in church, the preference of choruses to hymns, the presence of long hair, emotionalism, gaps in Bible knowledge, domestic tangles, youth (or old age), traditionalism, trendyism, speaking in tongues, enthusiasm, and a dozen other 'offences.' In three ministries which have seen many added to church membership, I have found that inculcating this attitude has been one of the essential keys to evangelism. Failure to do so accounts more than anything else for churches that I see dying out. A gospel that mouths God's forgiveness but does not enable Christians to forgive one another simply will not be heard, for it cannot be seen.

THE DECISION-MAKING PROCESS

So far Matthew 18 has pinpointed personal relationships. But a wider dimension is now introduced. The 'you' and 'your' (singular) of verses 15–17 are replaced by 'you' (plural) from verse 18 onwards. The same happens to the related verbs. It has become 'you all' as our American friends say. The *church* is specifically mentioned — and in the most solemn of circumstances.

> If he will not listen ... tell the whole thing to the church. Finally if he will not listen to the church, treat him as though he were a pagan or a tax-collector.
>
> Matthew 18:17

The church has come together. Nonconformist pioneers used the significant phrase 'the gathered church.' The practice, if not the full theory, seems now to be widely accepted by Anglicans as well (especially in front-line mission situations). The committed community is what we are aiming for, and what Jesus seems to portray here: the church.

'Tell the whole thing to the church' — notice. Not the Pope. Quoting the other 'binding and loosing' passage in Matthew 16, the Catholic church points to Peter, and thus to the Bishop of Rome. Not the hierarchy. Episcopal churches point to the other passage in John 20 addressed to all of the apostles, and claim church government through their successor-bishops. Not the church court. John Calvin got as far as Matthew 18, and then interpreted 'the church' of verse 17 and 'yourself' of verse 18 as the leadership meeting in solemn session; the eldership. But Jesus did not say that. There is not a hint of it. *The church* binds and loosens, and all its members agree on earth about what they hope to see ratified in heaven.

This is the doctrine of church-meeting government, reintroduced to the church by the first Separatists (see chapter 5) and maintained by Congregationalists, Baptists, and many independent and evangelical churches and which finds different but real

26

expression within Anglicanism. It has fallen on hard times and into keen criticism, and what it has often developed into deserves it. But the original will bear a lot of examination.

The principle is clear, *Christ's presence constitutes the church*. Here is the uniqueness of the church, and its difference from all other institutions. People are held together by common hobbies and interests (tennis club, philatelic society, football supporters' club). They are held together by common concerns (prevention of cruelty to children, banning nuclear weapons). They meet on the ground of a common social experience (working-men's club, law society). They work for a common cause (the Conservative Party, the United Nations Association). They are bound by a common culture (Muslims, motor-bike gangs). But the church is unique. It meets around the shared experience of the living person of Christ. Verse 20 tells us so: 'For where two or three come together in my name, I am there with them.' Apart from the vivid reminders about mutual forgiveness which follow, this is the end of the great discourse, and the conclusion of Christ's last charge to his disciples in Galilee.

The rest of the New Testament makes it clear what he meant. *The gift of the Holy Spirit is the presence of Jesus.* Released from physical restraints and ascended into heaven, Jesus is everywhere present in spirit (John 14 and 16). The story of the Acts is the illustration. Changes include a new approach to decision-making. 'The Holy Spirit and we have agreed not to put any other burden on you ...' they wrote calmly and breathtakingly after the church had met in discussion and debate (Acts 15:28). Read the Book of Acts as a guide-book on decision-making, and you will find that the Holy Spirit is more often associated with decisions and guidance than with power in witnessing!

That is what church-meeting is all about. The living Christ is with his people. They gather 'in his name': that means they invoke his presence, for by the power of the Holy Spirit, his name is his presence. 'In the name of Jesus Christ of Nazareth ... get up and walk' (Acts 3:6).

They 'gather in his name'; that means they act consistently with his character and in harmony with his nature: 'That in all things he might have the preeminence' (Colossians 1:18, AV).

They gather 'in his name'; that is they know they have immediate access to God the Father through him (the particular thrust of verse 19 in our key-chapter is — 'Agree ... pray ... it will be done').

They 'gather in his name' and the Sanhedrin-Below answers to the Sanhedrin-Above. Heaven moves in response to earth's needs. Christian people pray and think and act—and God's energy is released on earth.

That is church discipline — for all and by all. In a later chapter we shall return to the sorry sight of what it has often become, but this is where church discipline begins. Christ meets with his church and reigns in his church.

How does it actually work? What are its main elements? How has it developed over the centuries? We shall look at some of the discoveries, some of the mistakes, some of the recoveries, and follow this by addressing the practical problems. What is the role of the missionary? The pastor? The overseas mission board? The church council? The elders and deacons? The church gathered together? How is the Bible effectual in discipline? What of the cultural clashes and the problems of permissiveness? Where does the Lord's Table come into it? Where does the authority lie? We shall examine some of these questions and, I hope, learn something from the answers.

Note

1. John Howard Yoder, 'Binding and loosing' in *Concern*, 14 (February 1967).

Part Two: The Principles
CHAPTER FOUR

Word in Action

I WAS preaching through that happiest and most attractive of books, Paul's letter to the Philippians. Week by week and section by section, we explored and enjoyed its truths and challenges.

I checked next Sunday's verses. They began not very promisingly, 'Euodia and Syntyche, please, I beg you, try to agree as sisters in the Lord' (4:2). Not a very meaty section at first sight, I thought. Perhaps I should skip it. But I looked again, and saw some fine possibilities. I got down to preparation.

That Friday, I heard of a sharp quarrel between two women in the church who were key workers in our effort to win the youth of a tough working-class district. Everyone soon knew about it. To preach two days later about two women in the church who fell out would be ridiculous!

I thought again. Maybe not so ridiculous after all. One of the great values of verse-by-verse expository preaching is this; it delivers the hearers from the treadmill of the preacher's personal fancies, and gradually gives them the word of God *whole*. Welcome or unwelcome, disturbing or comforting, there it is. And here was a fine example of the virtue of that practice. Everyone knew the point we had reached in Philippians. Most people knew that I had my Sunday morning sermon ready by Thursday. No one could accuse me of being too personal, or of rigging a sermon to score a point.

So I preached it. There were some round eyes when I read the lesson. There was keen attention when I began the sermon. I ploughed on. Two women, leaders in the church at Philippi, had quarrelled. It was important enough to mention in the Bible (what a way to get your name read in thousands of churches!). Obviously, God views very seriously a rift between Christians. Why is that? And how can such quarrels be settled? Paul tells us.

First, *we are all members of God's Family*. Verse 1 says,

'Brothers, how I miss you! How happy you make me, and how proud I am of you.' We belong to each other. Think how many things bind us together. The blood of Christ shed for us, the Spirit of God given to us, the gospel brought to us, a common destiny; we are one family. 'Euodia and Syntyche...sisters in the Lord.'

Second, *our existence as a family is evidence for the gospel*. These people were Paul's 'joy and crown' (4:1, AV). He could point to them. The vindication of Paul's gospel, the seal of God upon its preaching, was the existence of these churches where barriers were broken and love prevailed.

Thirdly, *that family is under attack*. 'Stand firm in your life in the Lord,' Paul goes on to say in verse 1. It is a military term, also used in the famous 'armour of God' passage. Satan seeks to sabotage the work of the gospel by dividing Christians. He is the real enemy.

Fourthly, *that family has as its principal business the service of the gospel*. 'They have worked hard with me to spread the gospel.' Paul is a little tongue-in-cheek. 'Working hard' is a military term too. 'In these early days you two were fighting as well — *but not each other!'*

Fifthly, *eternity is involved in this family life*. 'Whose names are in God's book of the living' (verse 3). The only thing that will matter when this world ends!

And a final point. Paul mentions these two women by name. But he never expresses any opinion about the rights or wrongs of their quarrel. He takes no sides. The quarrel itself is the greatest wrong. They are sisters. They are to make it up as sisters.

So I preached it. There was no need for a personal application. The two went straight to each other after the Benediction, and apologised to each other. The whole church was strengthened in its understanding of family fellowship.

ANOTHER ANTIDOTE

I tell that story at some length, because it illustrates a factor forever recurring in church life. The word of God, constantly and carefully and consecutively expounded, has an enormous healing power. Many potential causes for church discipline will never develop but will be quietly dealt with in embryo, as the Spirit takes the word and applies it to the people's hearts. We should expect it. 'All Scripture is inspired by God and is useful for teaching the truth, rebuking error, correcting faults, and giving instruction for right living' (II Timothy 3:16). In other words, the Bible teaches us what to believe, what not to believe, how not to behave, and how to behave (a useful sermon outline in itself!).

Notice the order. What we believe decides how we behave. The negatives of rejecting error and wrong behaviour are an essential part of the process. This ongoing process of purging-through-the-Word is an absolute essential of every church's healthy development. 'You have been made clean already by the teaching I have given you,' said Jesus to his first disciples at the end of his earthly ministry (John 15:3).

Because I have enjoyed a measure of 'success' in three successive growing and multiplying churches, people often ask me what was the secret. There have been varying constituents. Enthusiastic evangelism in one. The presence of many students and a renewal emphasis in another. Mobilisation of lay leadership and training of personal witnesses in another. But one feature they all had in common, and I give it without hesitation as THE factor: *systematic, doctrinal, practical, expository preaching of the word of God*, from almost every book of the canon. It was given with joy, because I love the Bible; with expectation, because I constantly found that it worked, and with authority because I handed it on as the sure revelation of the Lord who wishes to be known and obeyed.

THE OPEN SECRET — WORD WITH POWER

Notice why it works so well. Good preaching is certainly a factor; Paul speaks of 'the foolishness of preaching' having a special part to play in God's purpose of fooling the wise and exalting the weak. Preaching has within it those particular elements of personality, experience, eye-ball to eye-ball encounter, which are most conducive to that special kind of communication necessary in sharing God's word. Nevertheless, the accent is not on preaching in itself, but on preaching *the Word of God*. I'm not sure that we would have defined Jesus' parables and epigrams and pithy sayings as formal 'preaching,' but they were word-of-God. Peter's and Paul's sermons would, I suspect, have won only moderate ratings in a modern homiletics course, but they were impregnated with God's word. I recall, incidentally, slightly cheating in the homiletics course which I took by correspondence for my Baptist ordination. The sermon subject set for that week happened to coincide with one I had actually preached the previous Sunday as a lay-pastor, so I simply sent in the notes as my assignment. The examiner gave me rather poor marks. He said I did not relate it sufficiently to contemporary life. The odd thing is that six different people that week had come to me personally and told me of their conversion through that sermon. I think six

31

conversions is pretty contemporary!

In the long run, the Bible is the only thing which God undertakes to charge with power. Other things he may condescend to bless, for his own purposes. This one we can *expect*. But I make the point again, that the content is more important than the method. In this area, the medium is certainly *not* the message! That is why arguments about the actual method (visual aids, drama, etc.) are missing the point.

HOW THE WORD OF GOD WORKS

How may the Bible be applied to the everyday life of the church, in correcting and healing power, so that discipline is ongoing and almost unconscious? *Expository preaching* must be rated first, I think, because of its very nature. My story about the two women illustrates the advantages. It is consistent, consecutive, all-embracing, most free of the preacher's personal prejudices and preferences. It disarms criticism and negative reaction in advance ('How can he be getting at me? He was up to the previous verse last week. It must be *God* who is getting at me. Perhaps I'd better do something.') It carries the balance of theory and practice, belief and behaviour, lesson and anecdote, encouragement and rebuke, narrative and parable, which the Bible itself naturally carries. After all, what is more pointed and powerful — an essay about adultery or the story of David and Bathsheba? A lecture on the church's duty to evangelise, or a cameo from the Acts of the Apostles?

Although I have welcomed and used various schemes (Operation Agape, One Step Forward, the Archbishop's Call to the Nation, the Baptist Union *Signs of Hope*, etc.) I have never found them quite as effective as the simple regular exposition. Because they are 'special,' people are immediately on their guard. You are going to nag them, they suspect. You are after something. But let them come weekly with their Bibles, eager and expectant, and you have them. So, without my needing to make personal approach, I have seen stealing stopped, immorality abandoned, family relationships healed, bitterness melted, marriages mended, quarrels ended, tight-fistedness turned to generosity, occult dabbling disowned, homosexuality subdued, vicious temper calmed — usually without my being aware of the offence until it had been dealt with, but sometimes after I have discovered or suspected it. That is antidote at work. To change the metaphor, it is church discipline launching a pre-emptive strike before the evil has become overt.

HITTING THE TARGET

However, expository preaching is no lazy man's tool (as some who do not practise it seem to imagine — 'you don't have to spend time and energy deciding on a subject'). For the *application* requires disciplined thinking and courageous action. The Puritans, those master-preachers, normally finished their sermons with a long list of 'uses.' For example, in a sermon on Christian Assurance, having expounded the text and the doctrine, the preacher would then finish something like this:

Use 1 If our salvation is now complete and assured, how grateful we must be to God who gave it. Begin and end every day by thanking God.

Use 2 If God promises to give 'the full assurance of faith,' how we should 'labour to make our calling and election sure.' What earthly pleasure, possession or prize can equal the sweet certainty of eternal life. We devote much time to them; how much more to this?

Use 3 Assurance is a divine gift. It is not to be taken lightly. No mere physical or emotional sense of well-being should be mistaken for this. Do you bear the marks of a child of God? Have you fled immorality? Do you shun idolatry? Have you delight in God's word?

And so on. A sermon often had six or seven such 'Uses,' each much more fully illustrated and emphasised than my example. Without needing to copy the style, every preacher needs to have this aim. It is simply *the search for relevance*; this is what must engage his attention. This is what differentiates a sermon from a mere essay.

The preacher must particularise. Victorian caricatures portray preachers as fulminating vaguely and all-embracingly against 'sin.' Whether they really did so, I cannot say. But the preacher who is serious about God's word as a route to holiness must talk about *sins* — the particular, not the general. We must name, analyse, examine the things against which Scripture warns us. We must explain why pride is the worst of evils, why sex outside marriage is against God's will, why the tongue must be bridled, and why the arrogance that attempts to squeeze God's truth into my little brain-pan will lead me into soul-destroying error.

Alexander Whyte was the great exponent of this kind of preaching at the turn of our century, and his published character-studies should be on every minister's shelf (and open on his desk) if we are to avoid either sentimental permissiveness or repulsive legalism. His seed-bed was the Old and New Testament, his references Bishop Butler, William Law and John Bunyan, and his special flair an almost frightening imagination. Whyte repeatedly exposed particular sins to the fury of God's holy law and the melting power of Christ's holy love.

Listen to a sermon on Cain, linked with John's words, 'Whosoever hateth his brother is a murderer.'

> It was an old superstition that a murdered man's body began to run warm blood again as soon and as often as its murderer was brought near it. And in that way they used to discover who the real murderer was.
>
> Now, just suppose that that was indeed so. How many men still living would begin to be all over with blood in your presence? The man sitting next to you at this moment would be like a murdered corpse.
>
> The preacher now standing before you, your mother's son; the very wife of your bosom, when she does not flatter and fawn upon you; your own son; your dearest friend. Yes; you would then be what Cain all his days was…. They would know, they would be horrified at what it meant, when their throats began to run blood as they passed you on the street, or as you sat eating and drinking with them at your table, or at their table, *or at the Lord's Table*.[1]

Starting from the words, 'Your brother's blood cries out from the ground' in the Genesis story, Whyte has taken us to Jesus' warning in the Sermon on the Mount on angry words, John's words about love and hatred between brothers, and Paul's warning about self-examination at the Lord's Table. This is applied ethical teaching, and preachers must train themselves and pray themselves into doing it.

Incidentally, Whyte's method also underlines the enormous power of *character-study* in the Bible. It is no accident that great areas of the Old and New Testament are taken up with detailed pursuit of character-development. God knows what he is doing when he portrays truth to us through the way people lived and behaved. The complications caused by Jacob's wheeling-and-dealing, the havoc produced in David's family by his adultery, the effect that Daniel's integrity and prayer-life had in a pagan court, the way that Peter's impulsiveness led him into false paths, the weakness of John Mark who was nevertheless given another chance (and grabbed it) … these inimitable examples of vice and

34

virtue are in the Bible for our use, and it is folly to neglect them.

In my childhood home, the people who cram the Bible's pages were so familiar that we discussed them at meal-tables, joked about them to underline a point, and took their example as warning or encouragement in a way which must have sounded extraordinary to an eavesdropper. They were as real to me as Aunt Ethel, the headmaster of my school, the radio announcer. This is what our preaching should produce.

TEACHING, SEMINARS AND SMALL GROUPS

Only in my most recent pastorate did I really grasp the difference between *preaching* and *teaching*. I had always been committed to the systematic preaching already referred to. Teaching, I had to learn, is something else which cannot replace preaching but is needed to supplement it.

Increasing numbers of our members were new converts. As new converts always do, they would make splendid progress — and then reveal some startling gap in their perception or practice. Their growth was patchy. Things we traditionalists took for granted, they had never heard of: like chastity, observance of the Lord's Day, or a disciplined home (I don't rate them as equal, but simply put them together because that is how it happened). Certain habits they simply did not think of giving up. I was startled when a man, already fruitfully witnessing to his faith, swore in my presence without batting an eyelid. Engaged couples asked my opinion about sex before marriage, purely as an interesting topic, not a clear moral issue. People previously involved in spiritualism or the occult were sometimes instinctively aware of the need to repent and renounce it, but sometimes were not; a passing reference to it in a sermon would bring them, startled and enquiring, to my door. Someone already helping in the Sunday school would land in a financial mess, and it would become evident that they needed not merely a hand-out from 'the needy-saints fund' (as my childhood church delightfully called it) but, more urgently, some instruction in household management and stewardship.

At the same time we had traditional members quite shocked at some of these things. Were we opening the church to a flood of permissiveness? Were these folk really converted? Was the pastor failing to preach a proper standard? ... and so on. Incidentally, some of the same dear people saw no incongruity in the fact that after forty years of faith *they* had no victory over bad temper or a complaining spirit, and did not even feel a conscience about gossip and uncharitable criticism! Class came into this a good deal. The things that grieved them were often working-class vices; the virtues they looked for were middle-class virtues; the vices they made no effort to overcome were middle-class vices. This, of course, was only true of some. There were others who rightly and consistently clung to biblical values in themselves and looked for them in others.

AUTHORITY AND DISCUSSION

But again — when I 'preached' these subjects, there was a mixed reception. Some topics are hardly appropriate for detailed examination in the pulpit before several hundred people. The preaching style does not lend itself to the qualifications, intimacies, exploration of motive and audience participation that are sometimes needed for these things. Try to teach in the pulpit, and you finish up with an essay, a dialogue, a seminar, a debate, or an experiment; all excellent things, but not what the pulpit is for. The authority disappears. The 'thus saith the Lord' is muted. God's law is to be listened to and obeyed, not debated. I recall a convert asking my 'opinion' on the occult, and then replying, 'Well, that's a Christian viewpoint, but I don't think I agree.' I had to say to her, 'But my dear, it *isn't* a viewpoint. God has forbidden it, and your only choice is to give it up.' She did, fortunately.

On the other hand, if we only provide formal preaching, and make no space for questioning, discussing and explaining, the 'authority' begins to sound like mere dogmatism. The pulpit becomes what it has often been accused of being — a coward's castle, six feet above contradiction. So our teaching programme was developed.

We had *day seminars for young people about to start university*. At least we could warn them of that appalling but indescribable sense of alone-ness when the warm supportive Youth Fellowship is replaced by a totally secular, atheistic and arrogantly materialistic atmosphere in which faith is an oddity, a curiosity indulged in by a tiny minority. I recall pressing a girl from a gentle Christian home to tell the sixth-formers what she had told me privately — how on her first entry to the hall of the college she was confronted by an exhibition about lesbianism, and her roommate asked her to go off somewhere for the evening whilst she had her boyfriend in bed for a couple of hours. We could give them some elements of Christian evidences and apologetics. We could warn them that denominational college chaplains might well be apostates themselves.

We had *instruction courses in family principles*. It was our own doctors in the fellowship who pushed for this, and we have rarely done anything so provocative, protective, stimulating, healing and upbuilding. We used Dr Dobson's *Focus on Family* films, with a well-stocked bookstall and discussion groups afterwards. We repeated the process at intervals, and saw the fruit for years afterwards as families learned to apply the lessons. We also found ourselves with some complex problems that we just could not handle!

We had *moral instruction for teenagers*. This is a sticky subject, and I confess to mixed feelings about it. I am not sure, whether the church youth leader is really the right person to give sex instruction to *the children of Christians*. Is that not the task of the parents? But what then of Christian adolescents with non-Christian parents?

The Christian approach to work is a hot topic. The old 'Protestant work ethic' still has a lot to be said for it. But it badly needs some adjustments in the light of mechanisation, crushingly repetitive work, computerisation and now the robot revolution. One of the most exciting weekends I have ever conducted (for the Baptist Men's Movement) was on this subject.

Linked to this should be *preparation for retirement*. I was appalled, in a town that was on the verge of becoming a Costa Geriatrica, to see how totally unprepared many Christians are for the pressures and problems of old age and retirement. This was directly responsible for several discipline problems of a painful kind. Battles between 'trads and trendies,' professional jealousy of the minister, shifts of power between retiring elders and newer recruits to the eldership … let us be frank and admit that they exist.

More than anything else, older members need to learn the role of prayer-partnership. Whilst some bemoan the fact that the church is leaving them behind and everything is changing, others find joy in being prayer-watchers. A pastoral visit to them involves feeding them with fuel for prayer, and listening as they share their insights from wider experience. I can think of several examples of such saints, like the elderly lady who watched the youth choir singing to a church full of teenagers, and said to me with shining eyes, 'I prayed that I would live to see the young coming to our church. They are not doing it the way I always imagined, but they are here, and it is God's work!'

Banks and business establishments now put on courses for their ageing employees to prepare them for retirement. They are taught how to prepare for leisure, how to eat on a smaller budget, how to obtain benefits from the welfare state, what to join, and how to promote attitudes that see retirement as a boon not a disaster. Churches would do well to emulate them, and train their members in growing old gracefully. Look harder at many of the 'discipline' problems that explode in dismissed or resigned pastors, division on the diaconate and disorder in the parochial council: what will you find? Retired Christians who have not learned to turn age into sanctified enthusiasm.

WHO DOES THE TEACHING?

Tasks like this cannot be left to the minister. Often a good pulpit-man will not prove to be an ideal leader of a seminar, or a suitable small-group trainer. One man alone cannot produce the time and energy to create appropriate courses. One of my churches had a full-time salaried worker in charge of teaching (coupled with personal evangelism). It was a great success. Usually he in turn taught other leaders so that it was not left exclusively to him either. Mission England (1984) did the churches a great service in supplying courses like *Christian Life and Witness*, of which we made heavy use. There is, of course, no reason at all why leaders should not buy courses prepared by other organisations. The aim is instructiveness and usefulness, not originality. Moreover our churches are full of people who, in their own areas of life, have far more knowledge, experience and skill than the professional pastor. Bankers, policemen, social workers, shop-stewards, businessmen, schoolteachers, doctors and nurses — here are the people who both need guidance in applied Christian living and have much to offer others in their specialist areas.

What is the difference between preaching and teaching? Preaching is given to the whole church, whilst teaching is given to specific small groups. Preaching deals with general principles, whilst teaching handles specific applications. Preaching is still best done as a monologue to which people listen, whilst teaching is a dialogue in which people join. Preaching emphasises authority and command; teaching majors on exploration and discussion. Preaching should start with Scripture and apply it to today's situation; teaching can start topically and find its way through to Bible examples. Preaching is the regular diet for the whole church; teaching is the occasional activity of people interested enough to gather together specially for it.

PREPARATION FOR MEMBERSHIP

The place where preaching and teaching most closely merge should be in membership preparation. Denominational differences obviously come in here, but whether it be by confirmation class, baptismal training, discipleship group, or church membership class, there must be a real sense of direction and a real determination to *teach what the Bible says*.

I have had the same policy for many years, gradually developing it for new situations. The pulpit presents gospel challenge and Christian principles — in the shape of Bible exposition. Though very occasionally making an 'open appeal' (what our American cousins refer to as an 'altar call') I much more often rely on the simple announcement, frequently made, that Enquirers' Classes are available — some already in action, and another about to begin. There have been times when four or five, with five members in each, have been in progress at once.

For years I have used an adapted form of John Stott's book *Your Confirmation* (Hodder & Stoughton, 1958) with its accompanying film-strips (by CPAS and Falcon) which translate the truths into a visual cartoon form. Three lessons on *Christian Beginnings* deal with conversion, assurance, and Christian growth. Three follow on *Christian Beliefs*, covering the person and work of God the Father, the Son and the Holy Spirit. *Christian Behaviour* follows, with lessons on the Bible (why we believe it and how we use it), prayer (worship, thanksgiving, confession, intercession and petition) and the Ten Commandments. I then replaced Stott's two lessons on Confirmation and Eucharist, with three lessons on Believers Baptism, Communion, and Privileges and Responsibilities of Church members (the latter including worship, service, prayer, church government, the church meeting, financial giving, the gifts of the Spirit, missionary vision).

At the time of their reception into membership, our people should be receiving their first antidotes to worldliness and indiscipline — by receiving the word of God, systematically taught.

THE WORD IN THE WORSHIP

When we formed a new branch-church a few years ago (now independent and flourishing) I introduced the Presbyterian custom of presenting the Bible at the beginning of the service. A deacon or elder appears, carrying a large pulpit Bible. The congregation stands, and the Bible is placed in the pulpit or on the lectern. Only then does the minister appear. It is an eloquent symbol; preaching and worship are to be subject to the written Word of God. The same principle is underlined at the cathedral where I often worship in Jerusalem. Two robed youths with large burning candles held aloft accompany the Bible as it is carried to the lectern. The entrance of God's Word gives light — and never more clearly than when God's worshipping people are gathered together.

Worshipping people; I emphasise that. Worship is literally worth-ship, giving God that which is his right and due. That includes the reverent, believing and obedient hearing of his Word. This is the reason for the typical high pulpit of the Protestant church building, and the ornate lectern of the more liturgical type of church. Public reading of the Bible (which is what Paul urged Timothy to give his best attention to (I Timothy 4:13) should be an essential part of corporate worship, designed to produce two particular effects — adoration of God and obedience to his standards. There is a great deal to be said for a voluntary lectionary. Its cycle of readings — Psalms, Old Testament, New Testament and Gospel — takes the congregation through the whole spread of Bible teaching in the pattern of the church calender. Used as the source of the *preaching* I find it is disappointing; there is no systematic opening up of the books of the Bible, and the sermons tend to take the set reading as a mere jumping-off place for a few ideas or pious thoughts. But used as material for *worship* (and reverence for it encouraged) it can have great moral effect. We should expect this to happen, and pray for it. Try to imagine the first-century congregation at Rome listening for the first time to Paul's just-arrived epistle!

The Psalms (sung, paraphrased, chanted, read aloud or put to renewal music) are full of moral instruction shaped for corporate worship. It is no accident or mere sentiment that plants the twenty-third psalm in almost everyone's mind, and that makes familiar to all phrases like 'he set my feet on a rock,' 'I will lift up mine eyes unto the hills;' 'my rock and my fortress,' and 'the angel of the Lord encampeth round about them that fear him.' *The Beatitudes* appear in many hymnbooks printed for reading aloud, with suitable responses. How about using that response, followed immediately by the prayerful singing of 'Blest are the pure in heart' or 'May the mind of Christ my Saviour'? Similarly, we have the Ten Commandments with parallel New Testament comment added, and the responsive refrain, 'Incline our hearts to keep your law.' Good Protestant Nonconformists are often afraid to include public confession and absolution in worship but this need not involve either priestcraft or a denial of the 'finished work of Christ,' as they sometimes suppose. When we look at the Lord's Table we will see that this makes something of the sort appropriate, if not imperative. Personally, I always employ 'we' and 'us' rather than 'you' in any form of absolution, to avoid any hint of priestcraft; together we are seeking that ongoing cleansing which John's first epistle tells us to pursue.

WITH HEART AND VOICE

What we sing, and how we sing it, has an effect on our worship. There is, I know, a superspiritual and puritanical attitude to music-and-words in some circles. I understand and respect it, but profoundly disagree with it. There is really no valid reason for allocating words-song-instrument-and-gesture to the 'old covenant' along with blood sacrifices and Aaronic priesthood. Sacred music is not in itself an appeal to the 'merely soulish' (whatever that means). It is not 'merely emotional' (as if emotion is something suspect, separate from the whole being — a thought totally alien to the holistic concept that lies behind the biblical view of man). A psalm chanted Anglican-style in a parish church stirs the deeps in someone brought up in a church school, for example. The Holy Spirit is touching again the subliminal level at which childhood moral truth has been taught *from the Word of God*. At the other extreme, when I worship in a 'messianic assembly' in Israel, I can see and feel how appropriate it is to sing out the psalms of David as the original words suggest, with stringed instruments, strong beat, tambourines, clapping and dancing. The latter I tend to watch as a smiling Gentile, rather than indulge in — but how right it feels, and how appropriate to *the words which God has given*.

Somewhere between the two extremes we have the magnificent paraphrases of Watts and Wesley which we now call traditional hymns, and the newer 'renewal songs' which are often simply the original words of the psalm. It is particularly ironic that traditional hymns and renewal songs have become rivals in many English churches.... I have had letters addressed to me reminding me reproachfully how many of each I had in last Sunday's service, as if one kind was a treasure from heaven and the other something close to a smutty joke. Both are treasures. Both are words from the Word of God. Both have music extraordinarily suited to the words. The congregation whose leader has tossed out the hymnbook in favour of exclusive use of an overhead projector is as bereft as the group that clings to *Hymns Ancient and Modern* and scorns *Songs of Fellowship*. Incidentally, point out

41

that we are singing Scripture (whether in hymn or song), and read a few lines of the original reference.

THE PRIVATE PLACE

There is one more thing we can do, to bring Bible to bear on Christian behaviour before it ever becomes a matter of 'discipline.' We can carefully teach our people to read the Word of God for themselves, in a daily, devotional, disciplined way. The 'new spirituality' that scorns Scripture Union daily readings or Navigators' memory courses as something legalistic should find no place amongst us. 'Thy Word have I hid in my heart, that I might not sin against Thee,' said the psalmist, and there is no substitute for that. Writers of daily notes give great attention to the relevance and application of their Bible passages. I know, I am one of them! What does this tell me about God? About myself? About a vice to avoid and a virtue to pursue? What should I go and do because I have read this? These are the questions posed daily, in one way or another.

A reader writes:

> I cannot begin to tell you what a difference it has made to use *Alive to God*. I am learning to ask God daily to teach me something new ... and to *expect* that he will do this ... and the joy is I am not disappointed. Some truly wonderful experiences have resulted in my own life as I am learning to listen to God and to become obedient to his voice.[2]

Learning to listen to God and become obedient to his voice; one could not better express the purpose and function of the Word in the Christian's life. Prevention is better than cure, the saying goes. Here is the way to reduce to a minimum the stern and sad aspect of church discipline, by making it largely unnecessary.

Notes

1.   Alexander Whyte, *Bible Characters (Old Testament)*, Oliphants, 1958.
2.   M.A., West Midlands, advertisement for *Alive to God*, Scripture Union, London, 1984. Used by permission of Scripture Union.

CHAPTER FIVE

The Table that Hurts and Heals

> The wounded surgeon plies the steel
> That questions the distempered part
> Beneath the bleeding hands we feel
> The sharp compassion of the healer's art
> Resolving the enigma of the fever chart.
>
> T.S. Eliot[1]

PAUL'S letter to Corinth contains some of the New Testament's most startling and solemn words. They have to do with our theme.

> If anyone eats the Lord's bread or drinks from his cup in a way that dishonours him, he is guilty of sin against the Lord's body and blood.... If he does not recognize the meaning of the Lord's body when he eats the bread and drinks from the cup, he brings judgement on himself as he eats and drinks. That is why many of you are weak and ill, and several have died.
>
> I Corinthians 11:27, 29–30

There is a startling sacramentalism here which rests very uneasily on good western protestant shoulders — especially if we are Nonconformists. A blunt realism associates so closely the eating of the bread and our attitude to the Lord's body, our right partaking and our experience of judgement or blessing. Almost every attempt at church discipline has involved banishment from the Lord's Table (temporary or permanent), as one of its more serious penalties. Paul goes a good deal further and maintains that the Table will exert its own discipline! Sin undealt with in the Corinthian church led to a misuse of the Lord's Table, and *'that is why'* some were ill and several had died.

Some commentators suggest that 'weak,' 'ill,' and 'died' are metaphorical phrases to describe spiritual decline rather than physical consequences. That is very doubtful, but in any case is hardly less solemn. The warning still remains, not merely that careless partaking of communion is to be deplored, but that it has dire repercussions. As a direct result of cause and effect, it leads to spiritual loss or physical harm. The Table can hurt as well as heal.

I have never forgotten a scene which I witnessed in the first year of my Christian life. The little assembly which broke bread together each Sunday morning contained some shaky characters, to put it mildly. One morning, as we sat in a circle and passed the bread and wine to one another, we reached that trembling sensitive moment of total rightness that can, in a time of open unstructured worship, be so obvious without any intervention of liturgy or leader. Then six of the members, sitting together, staged a protest, obviously preplanned. With stern and angry faces they each refused the bread and cup with a sharp gesture, and sat stonily silent. Of course the atmosphere was ruined, and at the very moment when hearts should have been caught up with Christ. We had just sung:

> Shut in with Thee, far far above
> The restless world that wars below

yet every mind was now agitated with questions and guesses. It emerged that the six people had some petty quarrel with the elders, partly on a matter of what constitutes 'worldliness' and partly because they felt they were as good as anyone else, and why should they listen to the elders anyway?

I was shocked and shaken. The sequel was solemn and instructive. Not one of the six survived as a practising Christian: within two years four of them had drifted into spiritual weakness and sickliness; the other two succumbed to very odd physical illness and died. Of course the story goes around in a circle. Was the failure in Christian living (even the illness) a contributory factor in the self-righteous protest? It certainly made an impression on me!

COMMUNION AT CORINTH

The Corinthian communion service was a remarkable thing; remarkable both for the importance attached to it and the irregularities which had crept into it. As the Christians gathered for communion they were very conscious of being a small

44

despised minority in a corrupt and depraved society. *Out there*, men and women feasted at pagan altars, and climaxed the feasts with horrible sexual licence. *In here*, they recalled a spotless sacrifice once made and never to be repeated, responding to it by offering themselves in love and obedience.

Out there, the demons were a grim reality, using the vague figures of non-existent 'gods' to batten on confused humanity and feed on its superstition and credulity. *In here*, Christ was a glorious reality, and communion with him was real.

Out there, a parody of fellowship was enjoyed, that sense of belonging to others for which the human spirit craves, and finds its equivalent in pub, club and secret society today, as it then found it in mystery-religion, cult or at shared orgy. *In here* the one loaf and one cup both symbolised and strengthened that oneness with each other and their common Lord within the mystical body of Christ.

They apparently made it a 'common meal,' each bringing whatever food and drink he could, to partake in the love feast. But there the irregularities began, or rather expressed themselves, since they were already present in the heart. Class distinction and social snobbery were shown, as the wealthy kept their expensive food to their own circle, and the poor watched hungrily and angrily. Sectarian differences between those who followed Peter, those who favoured Apollos and those who preferred Paul, were betrayed in the same unholy huddles that denied the unity of the body. Some who came to the table of the Lord had not broken with the demons; social pressure, lingering paganism and careless libertarianism still led them to pagan sacrifices, and they were unable to distinguish the holy Supper from a godless feast. Drunkenness and immorality, so characteristic of the pagan cultures around them, still lingered unrestrained (see I Corinthians 5:1 and 11:17–21).

It was this that God judged. 'Eating and drinking unworthily' (11:29) was what brought judgement to them. Notice it is the adverb, not the adjective. We often get them confused. They were not chastised for being *unworthy* (adjective describing themselves) for who amongst us is ever worthy? 'We are not worthy so much as to gather up the crumbs from under your table ...' We come, indeed to say, '*Thou* art worthy.' Rather, they came *unworthily* (adverb, describing their actions at the table). The things they did at the Feast, and the attitudes they showed, were a denial of his body (11:29). To 'not discern the Lord's body' (AV) does not mean (as I used to imagine as a child), failing to hold the correct interpretation of what happens to the bread;

how it can be described as his body, whether 'real presence' or 'mere memorial' or even whether transubstantiation is involved. The 'body' referred to is surely *the body of the church*, as in 10:17:

> Because there is the one loaf of bread, all of us, though many, are one body, for we all share the same loaf.

That body was 'not discerned', for the well-off feasted and ignored their hungry brethren, the semi-idol-worshippers polluted the feast and soiled their innocent brethren, the immoral dragged fellow-Christians into a forbidden relationship, the heretical disbelievers in resurrection muted the united witness, and the quarrelsome sectarians tore apart the church.

In other words, the very kind of offence which disrupts the church, denies its fellowship and destroys its witness, therefore requiring discipline, is the very kind of offence which was both shared and judged at the Communion Table in Corinth.

WHAT THE TABLE SAYS — FIRST THERE IS FELLOWSHIP

The reasons are fairly obvious. The Lord's Supper combines so many features that are at the heart of the Christian gospel and the church fellowship. In its proper celebration, we will find the positive blessing which is the preventative and antidote for church disorders.

We have seen already, *there is fellowship*. The one loaf symbolises the one body of the church, as well as that physical body in which Christ offered himself on the cross. Not for nothing do we 'share the peace' with our fellow Christians. The early church historian Irenaeus, incidentally, maintained that it was no true eucharist where the kiss of peace was not shared. In that act we come back once more to Matthew 18, the reconciled fellowhip, and also to Matthew 5:23–24: '… you remember that your brother has something against you, leave your gift there in front of the altar, go at once and make peace with your brother.' Every communion should include time for quiet contemplation ('everyone should examine himself,' as Paul will say in 11:28). Then either a public cover-all confession and declaration of pardon liturgically, or an exchange of the peace (or preferably both) should follow. Where the renewing work of the Holy Spirit is evident, this course should be expected to lead to changed attitudes.

A courageous Baptist pastor in a nearby church to me (enjoying much of spiritual renewal) once came down from the Table at this point and apologised to his wife for having lost his temper with her that morning. With that kind of leadership and attitude, offences will be nipped in the bud. It is, of course, an ongoing principle of the East African Revival. This very attitude is encouraged in every communion liturgy, and the fact that there it is expressed more formally does not have to make it any less real.

REMEMBRANCE OF HIM

'Do this in memory of me' (11:24). There is the sacrament at its simplest. We need the constant reminder of — 'all our redemption cost, all our redemption won.' The physical sight of bread and wine, the physical act of breaking and pouring, the physical exercise of eating and drinking, focus our memories on the price paid for our forgiveness, and who it was that paid it. Forgiveness, notice. Again and again at the Lord's Table, in remembering the cost, we are reminded of the seriousness of sin. Then how can I ever think lightly of sin again?

'Ye are not your own,' wrote Paul, 'for ye are bought with a price' (I Corinthians 6:19–20, AV). So I am. Then I can never live again as if it were my own life, with which I can do what I like.

PROCLAMATION OF PARDON

'Every time you eat this bread and drink from this cup you proclaim the Lord's death.' This 'proclaim' of 11:26 is the 'preach' of 9:14 ('Those who preach the Gospel should get their living from it'). We are all, in a sense, evangelists at the Table.

Christians differ on how private or public the Communion should be. Certainly indiscriminate partaking should be avoided. Many Anglicans are profoundly unhappy at the occasional spectacle of a certain type of parishioner taking Communion at Easter, never to be seen again until Christmas. This practice has no support in the intention of the Prayer Book. On the other hand, strict Nonconformists who get wildly excited about the danger of an 'unconverted' chancing to take Communion, are quite misunderstanding the warning which Paul sounds. That warning is addressed to Christians. A believer wrongly communing is a more serious matter than an unbeliever mistakenly taking part. Some believe that the Lord's Table is a 'saving ordinance;' its proclamation should be expected to bring people to saving faith. The Wesleys believed this and often saw it happen. It seems appropriate that the unconverted should be present, but not partaking, and I have never found any great difficulty in arranging

47

that if there is the will to do so.

More than once I have seen an enquirer's face light up in the course of the service; faith has dawned, and he or she has taken the bread and cup, there and then, for the first time. I recall a Hindu student, long held back by fear of the demons, suddenly coming to decisive commitment before my eyes, and grasping the cup with shining face. More often, I have seen Christians restored from some path of disobedience. One such was unrecognisable as a Christian and unknown to be one, because of deep bitterness of spirit through suffering the consequences of disobedience. She attended church for months and then one day at Communion the light dawned, tears flowed, silent confession and restoration took place, and she reached out for the bread and wine. They had declared pardon to her. Another Christian woman, trapped in psychological illness and neurosis, grasped the meaning of pardon as wine was being poured out, and felt (she afterwards said) that it was pouring over her head and shoulders, washing away the resentment and fear. She was healed, emotionally and spiritually.

EXPECTATION OF HIS COMING

'Christ has died, Christ is risen, Christ will come again' (Anglican *Alternative Service Book*). Here is our faith and expectation. 'You proclaim the Lord's death *until he comes*' (11:26). He has left us this memorial feast to bridge the gap between his ascension and his glorious return.

Christ's return should be often stressed, and not left to offbeat fringe groups. The purpose is not to become experts with prophetic charts, linking the Common Market with the ten toes of Daniel's image (or whatever). Peter asks, 'What kind of people should you be? Your lives should be holy and dedicated to God, as you wait for the Day ...' (II Peter 3:11–12). When he comes — will I want him to find me like *this*? There is a spur to consecration and discipline, if ever there was one.

COMMUNION WITH OUR LORD

All of this, with the promise of Christ's presence, justifies the word *communion*. We do not merely remember him; we commune with him. 'With joy we come to meet our Lord.' This accounts for the note of joy constantly repeated in the early chapters of Acts. Frequently felt then, and often sadly absent now, is the breathless sense that 'He is here: the Master familiar and loved.' But the realism cuts both ways. Paul recalls ancient Israel. When the people ate part of the sacrifice they had offered, they were united to the altar, so to speak (10:18). This is grimly true, in another sense, of the altars of paganism.

> What is sacrificed on pagan altars is offered to demons, not to God. And I do not want you to be partners with demons. You cannot drink from the Lord's cup and also from the cup of demons; you cannot eat at the Lord's table and also at the table of demons.
>
> I Corinthians 10:20–21

There is a note of real conflict here.

> Do we want to make the Lord jealous?
> Do we think that we are stronger than he?
>
> I Corinthians 10:22

It is a dangerous thing to provoke God's anger, unless (Paul adds sarcastically) we think we can withstand his power and resist him. 'Shall we rouse almighty wrath? Are we a match for God?' (Matthew Henry).

There is such a thing as real communion with evil. Analogous to it in some ways, but the opposite of it, there is real communion with good, and with God.

> The cup we use in the Lord's Supper and for which we give thanks to God: when we drink from it, we are sharing in the blood of Christ. And the bread we break: when we eat it, we are sharing in the body of Christ.
>
> I Corinthians 10:16

This is a high view of the sacrament indeed. It is acutely appropriate, in both the new churches of the East and the older churches of an apostate West. The occult is real and powerful. I suspect that there are more witches in England than Baptist ministers. It is likely that more people read horoscopes than read the Bible. In Africa and Asia animism and witchcraft are part of the very air we breathe. Our conduct of Communion, the spirit in which we prepare and approach it, the sense of the holy Presence prevailing at it, should be such that demonism cannot breathe there.

ANTIDOTE, MEDICINE AND SURGERY

What should happen at Communion, then? The Lord's Table should act as an antidote. 'The body of Christ preserve your body and soul unto everlasting life,' our liturgical friends say as they dispense the bread. If we have prepared ourselves before we come, searched our hearts at the behest of the apostle in the Bible and the president at the Table, and seen something of Christ by faith, through word preached, memory stirred and sacrament received, then our lives should be preserved from infection and renewed in obedience. The service should have such expectation built into it.

Here is medicine, too. There has been disobedience? Then we seek healing here, in faith and vision. We should be helped to expect it. None of this is very likely to happen if the Lord's Supper is a voluntary extra, tacked on to the regular worship, offered to the people keen enough to stay after the majority has responded to the appeal to go home (that is barely an exaggeration, in some circles).

Sometimes, sadly, surgery is necessary. It should always be when all else fails. The sickness has not responded to antidote or medicine. The offence is stubbornly continued. Appeals and warnings are unheeded. Then excommunication cuts off the offender from all fellowship and therefore from Communion. Or the 'lesser excommunication' of withdrawal of Communion only (and for a short period) may be employed.

LESS THAN EXPULSION

This seems to be the implication of certain scriptures, such as I Corinthians 5:11. 'You should not associate with....' By 'not associating' does Paul mean full expulsion from membership (for a wide variety of offences including 'greed' and 'slander'!) or does he mean something like 'Don't cultivate their friendship; don't encourage them socially'? In fact, Paul continues 'Don't even sit down to eat with such a person.' Roland Allen, pioneer in so much missionary thinking, suggests that this is simply an exhortation to other Christians to use their private influence by 'the silent rebuke of avoiding their company.' Maybe so. But that could hardly *not* include their company at the Table of tables. II Thessalonians, incidentally, gives laziness and disinclination to be taught, as further reasons (3:6).

In the Third World churches, such discipline often cuts deeper than in our western culture. The Lord's Supper has a very concrete healing significance. To be cut off from it means to be starved of God.

Clearly, there are dangers in this. I have heard a perceptive man complain that, in his observation, this policy turns the Communion Service into a procession of the righteous who, by their permitted presence there, announce that they have not committed adultery this month — or at any rate, that they have not been caught. Yet there is plenty of evidence to suggest that suspension can have a positive effect. Temporary suspension from the Table has a long and honourable history amongst those who have practised it. 'Sitting Back,' I recall, was an occasional custom in the Brethren Assemblies of my youth. The offender attended, but sat on the back rows and did not receive the bread and wine. I do not recall any being driven away. I do recall the joyous welcome back they were given within a few weeks.

The Church of Scotland, in Calvin's tradition, long practised 'fencing the table' — a course of solemn heart-searching sermons attended by all who hoped to communicate next time. Tickets were then issued by elders who visited them and observed the effect. It was an adaptation of Calvin's Geneva, where its purpose was,

> to watch over the practice of received doctrine, to recall the hesitant, to admonish the weak and the fallen, in order to win them back rather than to frighten them away.[2]

It is a definition that takes some bettering.

How, then, can the Lord's Table function as the place that both hurts and heals, for the better health of the body of the church?

A lot will depend on the teaching given and the expectation engendered. An understandable reaction against magic sacramentalism has led some evangelicals to insist that nothing actually *happens* in the sacraments. (I have actually heard a Baptist warn his baptismal candidates — 'It is only a symbol. Don't expect anything to happen!' Hardly what the Bible says!) We must get away from that attitude. Communion must not be regarded as an optional extra. There should be some structure to it, some time given to it, and some preparation put into it. Bible teaching should accompany its administration. The teaching should focus on the glory of Christ's person and his 'finished work' at the cross, the benefits of our redemption, the relationship of holy living to God's calling. The constituent parts of the meaning of the Table should be stressed at intervals, now emphasising one, now another — each linked with the believer's experience, progress, growth, chastisement, challenge, etc.

The structure should always include some emphasis on preparation of heart, confession of sin, adjustment of life, and guarding of the fellowship. I have often encouraged people in silent prayer to look for signs of wrong relationship (impure thoughts, unforgiven quarrels, neglect, silent criticism, gossip, etc), to confess it immediately to God in silence, and to promise him action as soon as the service is over—a letter written, a debt paid, a quarrel settled, an apology made. Paul's Corinthian warning should be read, at least sometimes.

Of course the height and climax of Communion must be in the contemplation of Christ, in his love and glory, and in renewed consecration. If people do not reach the Dismissal and Benediction with warmed hearts, shining faces, shamed consciences and renewed dedication then we should be asking God where we have got it wrong.

Notes

1.   T.S. Eliot, 'Four Quartets' from *Collected poems 1909–1962*, London, Faber & Faber, 1963, p201. Reprinted by permission of Faber & Faber Ltd.
2.   Jean Calvin, *Institutes of the Christian Religion*, ed. J.T. McNeill, trans. F.L. Battles, Philadelphia, Westminster Press, 1960; London, SCM Press, 1961, Book II: 'The Discipline of the Church.'
3.   Alan Redpath, *The Royal Route to Heaven: A Commentary on First Corinthians*, London, Pickering & Inglis, 1965.
4.   Charles Hodge, *Commentary on First Corinthians*, reprinted London, Banner of Truth Trust, 1958.

CHAPTER SIX

Grasping the Nettle

THE English phrase 'grasping the nettle' comes from the alleged fact that if you take hold of a stinging nettle with a good firm grip it does not actually hurt you. I have never put it to the test. I greet it with the same caution that I give to the claim that if you look straight in the eyes of a savage dog that is advancing on you, it will slink away. 'Let sleeping dogs lie' is a slogan more to my taste when it comes to canine chums.

Nevertheless, when we move from metaphor to reality, it must be done. When the Word has been taught and applied in public and in private, when the Sacrament has been ordered as it should, with all its holy influence, there is still a third step to take in preserving the witness and life of the church. 'If someone is caught in any kind of wrongdoing, those of you who are spiritual should set him right' (Galatians 6:1). The nettle has to be grasped. The dog has to be looked in the eyes. And if it is done with the gentleness and self-awareness that Paul goes on to promote, perhaps they will not sting or bite so very badly after all. 'You must do it in a gentle way. And keep an eye on yourselves, so that you will not be tempted too' (Galations 6:4).

I recall putting off one such action as long as I could. It was a matter of foolishness rather than sin; a relationship that 'caused talk' in my northern church. Because the two people were innocent but stubborn, their attitude was 'Let them talk' — even 'Let's give them a bit more to talk about.' All of the eldership were quite clear about two things — the people must be spoken to, and the minister rather than the elders should do the speaking!

I was praying about it in the vestry of the empty church, when I heard footsteps outside, glanced through the doorway, and saw the very man I was praying about. Unless I was prepared to make a mockery of my own prayer, I was trapped — now was the moment. Taking a deep breath, I invited him in and said my piece. He looked at me steadily in silence for a long minute, and then said, 'You are quite right, Don. I will never go there again.' The nettle was grasped, and it did not sting. Ever since, I have watched with joy the steady growth and leadership of that man.

A much more difficult problem arose in a southern church. The relationship was indeed a guilty one, and the harm being done was great. Leading families in the church were involved. In that case, once I promised God in agonised prayer (and after too much delay) to 'handle it today,' he himself stepped in with a good deal of drama. A car crash at the moment I was praying caused a shaken sinner to face eternity for a few minutes. The moment I made the accusation (a few hours after the crash) he confessed and abandoned the sin, and that was the end of it. My hands were intact that time, too.

For church discipline is both a demand and a provision of God. If we use it rightly, God will make it a blessing to both parties. He does it with the Word preached and the Sacrament administered; he will do it with this, too.

THIS HURTS ME MORE THAN IT HURTS YOU

That certainly does not guarantee that there will never be pain. Some of the Corinthian converts savaged Paul when he exercised discipline. 'I wrote to you with a greatly troubled and distressed heart,' (II Corinthians 2:4). Even when it was eventually accepted, there was pain in that, too, for Paul. 'Make room for us in your hearts. We have wronged no one' (7:2). The old tag about the schoolmaster caning the youngster with the words, 'This is going to hurt me more than it hurts you' (I always suspected *that* one too!) really is true in church discipline; those who inflict it shed the most tears.

Pain, too, for the recipient. 'Now, however, you should forgive him and encourage him, in order to keep him from becoming so sad as to give up completely' (2:7). And, of course, there is pain for the whole church. 'See what God did with this sadness of yours: how earnest it has made you, how eager to prove your innocence. Such indignation, such alarm, such feelings, such devotion …!' (7:11).

I have never forgotten the occasion in my youth when the elders asked non-members to leave after Communion, and then announced sadly that an engaged couple were expecting a baby. They were to 'sit back' until the baby was born; attending, but not receiving Communion. The man who announced it was in tears, the congregation wept, and the couple wept. I believe those tears were sweet to God. When, half a lifetime later, two of my own converts came to tell me of the same circumstances, I found myself sitting and crying unaffectedly. They were first shocked, and then visibly came to realise, as they had not grasped before, what they had done.

So the nettle does sometimes sting after all — but it still has to be grasped. How can we set about grasping it? And what specific nettles need to be grasped?

OCCASIONS OF CHURCH DISCIPLINE

The New Testament is nothing if it is not specific. *Sexual sin* is to be regarded in a very serious light indeed.

> I am told that a man is sleeping with his step-mother! ... You should be filled with sadness, and the man who has done such a thing should be expelled from your fellowship ... I have in the name of our Lord Jesus already passed judgement on the man who has done this terrible thing. As you meet together, and I meet with you in my spirit, by the power of our Lord Jesus present with us, you are to hand this man over to Satan for his body to be destroyed, so that his spirit may be saved in the Day of the Lord.
>
> I Corinthians 5:1–5

This, of course, is the case whose 'tears' we have already been looking at. So it did lead to repentance and restoration — eventually. The most solemn words are used. Notice the name, power and presence of Jesus invoked and involved; this is an outstanding example of the Matthew 18 principle at work. Notice how the whole church is implicated ('You should be filled with sadness ... as you meet together') as well as the leadership ('I have already passed judgement').

Why is sexual sin so specifically a case for discipline?

It soils the whole fellowship. Paul makes it clear. Sexual misbehaviour is never a matter of 'my business and no one else's.' It involves a watching world: 'It is being said ... I am told' (5:1). It always will be talked about. Indeed, Paul uses a strong phrase — 'it is being talked about everywhere.' The city was ringing with the story. I reckon that one adultery or 'affair' undealt with but publicly known, will put a local church's evangelistic witness back five years.

It affected the church internally, too. Paul saw in the congregation's cheerful tolerance of this offence a horrifying sign of inner disease in the church. 'How, then, can you be proud?' (5:2). Something was badly wrong. Instead of the church permeating Corinth, the city was permeating the church. The standards were falling. We see this problem widespread in the 1980's of course. We are no longer shocked as we once were. The insidious propaganda of permissiveness has had its effect: 'You know the saying, 'A little bit of yeast makes the whole batch of dough rise.' You must remove the old yeast of sin so that you will be entirely pure' (5:6–7).

It affects the Son of God. With horrifying logic Paul says later in this letter what none of us would dare to say, were it not in the Bible. Sex involves the whole being, not just the body. Two people who 'make love' truly become 'one.' But the Christian is already mystically 'one' with Christ. So:

> You know that your bodies are parts of the body of Christ. Shall I take a part of Christ's body and make it part of the body of a prostitute? Impossible! Or perhaps you don't know that the man who joins his body to a prostitute becomes physically one with her? The scripture says quite plainly, 'The two will become one body'. But he who joins himself to the Lord becomes spiritually one with him.
>
> I Corinthians 6:15–17

It defiles the temple of the Holy Spirit. God does not now live in temples of stone and wood, 'holy places' in geographical locations. His dwelling place, by his Spirit, is the body of the church, and the body of the individual Christian.

> Avoid immorality. Any other sin a man commits does not affect his body; but the man who is guilty of sexual immorality sins against his own body. Don't you know that your body is the temple of the Holy Spirit, who lives in you?
>
> I Corinthians 6:18–19

A cause for concern and action. We have rightly moved away from the shocked, scandalised, almost prurient reaction to sexual sin which sometimes characterised the church in the past. 'Fallen woman,' 'divorced woman,' and such phrases suggestive of moral leprosy are fortunately not widely used amongst us any more. Perhaps the reaction has gone too far. It was suggested in a fine Christian magazine recently that 'God forbids it' is no longer a simple line sufficient to take with our young people. That rather depends on how real God is to them, and how confident they are that the speaker is really reflecting what God says! I would have thought it was exactly the line we need to take — along with the spelling out of *why* God forbids it. When necessary, discipline should be exercised *with both purposes in view* ... to restore the offender and to cleanse the church.

Some descending scale of severity seems necessary from the very logic of the scriptures involved. Persistent adultery and homosexuality should surely lead to dismissal. I use both terms in the strictest sense; adultery is intercourse between two people, at least one of whom is married to someone else; homosexuality is intercourse between two people of the same sex. In each case, I take it that the physical act is the crunch. Anything less than that (a dangerous relationship which needs to be cooled off) requires warning and action, but not necessarily excommunication. Persistent immorality of an unmarried person in a series of 'relationships' would also require the severest action.

What of a relationship which is voluntarily confessed through the working of conscience and the effect of God's Word? I would see no need to share this more widely than amongst those to whom it is confessed; the very confession surely indicates repentance and the beginning of restoration. What is needed now is pastoral care and advice to ensure that it does not happen again. If the offenders are involved in some public church work, I would suggest a period of withdrawal from it.

What of a couple already engaged to be married? If they find that the girl is pregnant and that alone has led them to confess, I would judge that they should bring forward their marriage date, step down from any public leadership and service in the church, and abstain from taking communion until they are married and the baby is born. The fact that they are stepping down should be discreetly made known; the reason will become obvious enough. The church's young people should have it explained to them that being engaged does not 'make it all right.'

On the other hand (and at the risk of being misunderstood!) I believe that their engagement does make a difference. They have committed fornication (to quote the ugly but frank word of the AV). But that is certainly not as serious as adultery, and nor is it the same as indiscriminate 'sleeping around' (to use the disarmingly gentle phrase now in vogue). As I understand Paul's words 'physically one,' what they have done is to consummate their marriage before they were wed. They are now in fact married, and should mark the fact by 'getting married' as soon as possible. This should be explained to them. They are now going to need a lot of practical support and help. Excommunication is the last thing they need; now is the time for restoration and rebuilding. But let us be clear; that involves repentance.

HANDING OVER TO SATAN

We still have to look at this grim phrase, as it is used in the context of immorality:

> You are to hand this man over to Satan for his body to be destroyed, so that his spirit may be saved in the Day of the Lord.
>
> I Corinthians 5:5

What does it mean? It is usually assumed to be a synonym for excommunication — the total expelling of the offender from the membership of the church (not just reprimand or temporary suspension from the Lord's Table). 'A forceful expression for the loss of all Christian privileges,' Hodge calls it. There are two spheres of life: God's kingdom and Satan's dominion. 'Out there' is the world we once belonged to, 'without hope and without God' (Ephesians 2:12), obeying 'the ruler of the spiritual powers in space, the spirit who now controls the people who disobey God' (Ephesians 2:2). Rather extreme words to describe fairly decent folk who don't happen to be 'born again'? Not at all. The power is at work. Reflect how millions of decent people embraced Nazism. Ponder how decent people plead in the name of liberty for an appalling flood of pornography to be released. Consider how a huge proportion of decent people dabble in spiritism, the occult, horoscopes, ouija boards, and so on — direct lines to the evil one. Count how many decent people are propagators of, or victims of, the widespread breakdown of family life. Notice how many decent people in a studio audience find blasphemy particularly funny. It is a world shaped by Satan, full of minds bent by the god of this world.

Full excommunication means stepping back into that world, with all the consequences of loss of fellowship, absence from the sacraments, the silence of God's Word preached, the loss of the mutual support of spiritual friends, the loss of the loving direction of leaders. Temptation will become more severe, the enemy's power more obvious. The logical outworking of the particular offence will be unrestricted. *Yet all of this is still with a view to restoration.* So, as Paul says, 'the flesh' suffers so that 'the spirit' might yet be rescued.

That may mean literal physical suffering of the body. Misbehaviour at Communion led to sickness and even death (I Corinthians 11:30). Ananias and Sapphira lost their lives (Acts 5:1–11). Of course that must come directly from God, as he disposes. There is not the slightest justification for Christian leaders applying physical or mental pressure on offenders.

Or it may mean, more often, that the circumstances and solemnity of the dismissal and what follows destroy the carnality which led to the offence.

> Expose him to the dreadfulness and loneliness and awfulness of the sin of which he is guilty ... put him out for the destruction of carnality, until he loathes the very thought of the thing which he is practising.[1]

> The contrast between a present experience of the things of Satan and the nostalgic recollection of the things of God might cause a revulsion of feeling and conduct.[2]

SUMMARY — THE SEXUAL DILEMMA

The whole subject is a painful one. On the one hand we live in a day of extreme sexual laxity, and of truly horrifying perversion. Pressure to 'conform' is enormous. Yet there is nothing new in this. It was precisely the situation in first-century Corinth. The time in England between the brief puritan ascendancy of Cromwell's day and the Great Awakening of Wesley's day was similar. The younger churches of the Third World are confronted by it. Asking leader after leader of churches in South America, Africa and Asia what is their biggest internal church problem, I almost invariably get the reply — 'immorality.'

On the other hand, there is danger in making immorality *the* sin above all others, of comforting those who sit in sin but not this kind, of encouraging Pharisaism and self-righteousness, of crushing the weak who are victims of a society which they did not build, or natures they did not ask for. Especially is there danger, in a frightened reaction to permissiveness, of making sex the one sin that is not covered by the cross; of making our churches more particular than God about the company we keep and the people we welcome. We must not forget that famous woman caught in adultery (John 8:1–11). Put those stones down!

I once asked an older minister whether moral lapse means that the offender can never again be a Christian leader. He looked at me silently for a moment, and then asked, 'Would you call St Augustine a Christian leader?'

A young man in training for the ministry confessed to me after a convention service that his fiancée was pregnant. Deeply convicted of his sin, he asked me, 'Have I permanently disqualified myself from the ministry?' That depended on the way he now acted, I suggested. 'Go straight home and confess this to your minister and your college principal. Put yourself under their discipline and cast yourself on their mercy. I believe the day could come when, from your bitter experience, you can minister to others.'

Whilst Augustine prayed, 'Lord make me chaste, but not yet,' he got nowhere in Christian service. There came a time when a prostitute of his acquaintance greeted him, 'Hello! Recognise me? It's *me!*' To which he replied, 'Yes, but it's not me.' Leadership lay ahead of him.

Notes

1. Alan Redpath, *The Royal Route to Heaven: A Commentary on First Corinthians,* London, Pickering & Inglis, 1965.
2. Charles Hodge, *Commentary on First Corinthians* (reprint), London, Banner of Truth Trust, 1958.

CHAPTER SEVEN

The Problem of Heresy

NEXT to immorality, the commonest and clearest cause for excommunication in the New Testament is *heresy*. It is the only other sin which merits the dark words, 'handing over to Satan.'

> Some men have not listened to their conscience and have made a ruin of their faith. Among them are Hymenaeus and Alexander, whom I have punished by handing them over to the power of Satan; this will teach them to stop their blasphemy.
>
> I Timothy 1:19–20

There is a current running throughout the New Testament of *definition and defence of the faith*. Modern churches have become so tolerant of every kind of belief, so theologically shapeless and so embarrassed by doctrine confused with dogmatism, that we constantly fail to take this biblical emphasis seriously.

Jesus and his apostles made assumptions that are almost meaningless in whole areas of modern church life, and even leadership. It is important to look at some of them.

1. Truth can be defined in words. A law has been given that sums up God's moral requirements in *words*. A Book has been given which Jesus regarded as the *Word* of God. The task of the apostles was to hand on the *words* of Jesus. They assumed a commonly accepted faith amongst the churches which could be summed up in *words*. Their last instructions as they approached death and left the church without their personal witness, were to cling to those verbal formulae. Paul says,

> 'Hold firmly to the true words that I taught you.'
>
> II Timothy 1:13

> Take the teachings that you heard me proclaim ... and entrust them to reliable people, who will be able to teach others also.
>
> II Timothy 2:2

Peter says,

> I know that I shall soon put off this mortal body ... remember these matters ... we have not depended on made-up stories (myths) ... we were there (eyewitnesses AV).
>
> II Peter 1:14–17

John says,

> Be sure to keep in your hearts the message you heard from the beginning.
>
> I John 2:24

Much modern Christianity says exactly the opposite. Truth is so vast that it cannot be put into mere words. God is so great that no verbal concept can be allowed to limit him or be supposed to exhaust the truth about him. This sounds very impressive, even very spiritual. Indeed it contains an important truth. But it *must* be balanced with the whole assumption of the Bible, which maintains that *truth can indeed be verbalised*. It is 'propositional'. It can be put into words which have a definite meaning.

2. Truth has been given by God.   The Bible presents itself as a revelation granted by God. He took the initiative and moved toward us. The Bible thus constantly uses phrases like 'God said ...,' 'the Word of the Lord came ...,' 'the Lord says ...' and indeed often presents statements in the first person coming from God 'I say ...,' 'my people ...' etc.

Nowadays the Bible is constantly presented as a book of religious genius, a collection of ideas about God, a record of man's search for the divine. So a clergyman in a broadcast recently made the cheerful assertion, 'The Bible is full of men's ideas about God — some are good and some are bad; we must learn to distinguish.' In the terms of what the Bible says about itself, this is sheer misrepresentation.

3. If one thing is true, then its opposite is false.   The Bible can sound very intolerant. It is the intolerance that is a part of absolute truth. If a certain medicine is the only possible antidote to a deadly disease, then the claims of certain other remedies are false. So Jesus and his apostles frequently warned of *errors* — not differences of opinion, but serious untruths. When Jesus said, 'I am the way, the truth, and the life,' he added the necessary corollary, 'No one goes to the Father except by me' (John 14:6).

The apostles warn of the dangers of being mistaken about the foundations of the faith. Do we get right with God by self-effort, by religious performance, or by casting ourselves by faith on the grace of God? A difference of opinion about that is not an interesting academic discussion but a matter of life and death.

> You are deserting the one who called you by the grace of Christ, and are accepting another gospel. Actually there is no 'other gospel'.
>
> Galatians 1:6–7

4. Satan is the author of error. 'It was some enemy who did this,' says the dismayed farmer in Jesus' parable, when he finds his cornfield half-full of weeds (Matthew 13:24–30). We are left in no doubt as to who the enemy is. From the opening scenes in Eden, Satan has worked to distort God's truth and deny his will.

> Anyone who denies this about Jesus does not have the Spirit from God. The spirit that he has is from the Enemy of Christ.
>
> I John 4:3 cf. Colossians 2:8

Someone who has to wrestle with false cults to free folk from their influence soon becomes aware of a spiritual conflict and a subtle foe.

5. The choice between true and false teaching is a spiritual and moral choice. It is often presented as an intellectual choice, a matter of academic integrity, or an expression of tolerance and open-mindedness. The Bible presents it quite differently. What do you *want* to believe? To whom do you *choose* to bow the knee (Colossians 2:6–7)?

Much of this sounds dreadfully dogmatic, uncharitable and legalistic to modern ears. We are deeply influenced by an educational system shaped on atheist-humanist suppositions. Everything is open to debate; nothing is absolutely true. Yet the Bible is clear. There is a standard of absolute revealed truth. Those who stray outside it need to be steered back in — or disowned if they will not be guided.

'Give at least two warnings ... and then have nothing more to do with him' (Titus 3:10). That instruction comes at the end of a great summary of the foundations of our faith. Paul was fighting on two fronts, against pagan gnosticism and judaising legalism. He did not see the church as a debating chamber where interesting theories are debated and discussed, but rather as a body of people committed to received truth. That was the common consent of the New Testament church. 'Fight on for the faith which once and for all God has given to his people' (Jude 3).

Expulsion was the drastic remedy, then, for serious doctrinal error. For what causes? Paul mentions again the two men who were 'handed over to Satan', in a later letter to the same church.

> Hymenaeus and Philetus ... have left the way of truth and are upsetting the faith of some believers by saying that our resurrection has already taken place.
>
> II Timothy 2:17–18

> Alexander the metal-worker did me much harm...he was violently opposed to our message.
>
> II Timothy 4:14–15

It sounds very like the development of a modern 'cult.' First, there is elaborate 'spiritualising' of a clear Bible teaching. (In Ephesus, they apparently explained away the physical resurrection as a metaphor for new birth or enlightenment, or some such.) Then comes an open breach, and the new teaching begins to deride and oppose the church's messengers.

IRREDUCIBLE MINIMUM?

There is a line then, beyond which denial or distortion of basic truth cannot be tolerated. Where is it drawn? Several New Testament passages are clearly meant to sum up the heart of the faith. Significantly, they are usually given in the context of combatting error.

To Corinth, Paul writes defending in great detail the death of Christ for our sin, his literal physical resurrection and the promise this holds of resurrection and eternal life for the believer (I Corinthians 15).

To Philippi, he addresses the famous lyrical passage that speaks of Christ's essential oneness with the Father, his great stoop to share our humanity, his death and subsequent exaltation (Philippians 2:6–11).

To Colossae, he writes of Jesus as the visible expression of the invisible God, his lordship over creation, his pre-existence before his earthly life, his headship of the church, his death as the way of reconciliation of mankind with God (Colossians 1:15–20).

References to Christian conversion make it clear that it is to be understood in terms of faith and conviction, as well as changed life. The description of the new birth in Titus 3:4–8 would provide material for a six-month series of doctrinal sermons!

ERRORS EXPOSED

Further clues are provided by Paul's vigorous attacks upon false doctrine. They regularly showed the same features.

Legalism denied the free grace of God and the perfect sufficiency of Christ, by insisting on circumcision, Jewish customs, certain religious observances as conditions of salvation. Jesus-plus-something-else was the saviour. Faith-plus-something-else was the requirement. Paul combats legalism in his letters to Rome and Galatia. Significantly, these were the writings that thundered around Europe in the sixteenth-century Reformation, gripped John Bunyan in the seventeenth century, and lit up Wesley's life in the eighteenth-century Awakening. Constant care is needed, for human nature is Pharisaical at heart; we want to save ourselves. Sacramentalism and social action both move in this direction today if they become replacements for the Gospel, rather than consequences of it.

Mysticism was the second threat to the New Testament churches. Well-meaning teachers tried to update the Gospel and make it more palatable to 'modern man' by accommodating it to the latest climate of opinion. As a result it denied the real humanity of Jesus, deriding the resurrection, and dabbled in the occult. Paul exposed it in writing to the Colossians and to Timothy at Ephesus. It all sounds very familiar. The church that marries the current climate of opinion will find itself widowed every time the climate changes. What is left is no gospel. A more evangelical form of mysticism is the search for endless wonders and experience, which shifts the centre of gravity from Christ, cross and conversion.

Antinomianism is the technical term for permissiveness in theological garb. Extol God's grace by giving him plenty to be gracious about. Sin in order that grace may abound. That was the siren call of first-century religious permissiveness. Its modern equivalent has been variously labelled South Bank theology and secular religion. Law and love are put in opposition, where the Bible puts them in alliance. It can take an evangelical form, too, judging by the current swing into morals-invented-for-the-moment. Paul's answer to all this is found in his letters to Rome and Corinth.

SOMETHING LESS THAN EXPULSION

The radical step of 'handing over to Satan' will not always be necessary. Indeed, full expulsion should be treated with great caution and imposed with great reluctance. In Thessalonica there was an exotic approach to unfulfilled prophecy and the promise of Christ's return. It led to unhealthy excitement and irresponsible living. Paul says of the ringleader, 'Take note of him and have nothing to do with him, so that he will be ashamed' (II Thessalonians 3:14–15). At Rome there were some who upset people's faith and caused agitation. His advice was, 'Watch out for them,' 'keep away from them' (Romans 16:17). This may simply mean, 'give them the cold shoulder if they won't be advised. Be wary of them. Don't let them take control of your informal groups.'

We all know the kind of enthusiast who leaps into the latest religious craze and makes himself a nuisance. It may be an emphasis all very well in its place, but blown out of all proportion. Speaking in tongues, a new idea about the end times, the latest author with a dramatic experience, a formula for solving every problem, the need to act against abortion ... whatever it is, it becomes, not merely a valid Christian insight (as it often is) but the totality of faith, diverting the Christian's attention from the central thrust of the church's ministry.

It is a great pity — but it does not merit expulsion, unless it leads to persistent division and organised defiance of the leadership.

There are other differences of opinion which, if we are to be guided by Scripture, should not be causes for expulsion. Spiritual gifts, the millennium, the place of modern Israel in prophecy, the precise implications of the doctrine of election, fine differences in church government: these are all causes for lively debate in our churches, but they should not be causes for either division or excommunication.

CREEDS AND CONFESSIONS

It is wise to have a clear confession of faith to fall back on. Otherwise a clever and persistent teacher of error may place the leadership in a difficult position. My first church accepted the fairly detailed Statement of Faith of the Fellowship of Independent Evangelical Churches. We read it out at an annual meeting of the membership, and all reaffirmed their commitment to it. I took care to cover its teachings in the course of each year, through the regular preaching. In that church I have no memory of a single example of false teaching raising its head.

My second church had the rather undeserved name of being worldly and liberal when I began. I never saw the evidence of it, and a stronger proclamation than perhaps they were used to became readily accepted. Baptismal teaching and the fairly frequent public use of a Scriptural Declaration of Faith in the *Baptist Hymn Book* kept foundation truths before the people, as the church membership grew and trebled in numbers.

My third church had some great oddities in its constitution and its membership, but I went with open eyes so could not complain. Here there were members (though not leaders) who denied some of the fundamentals, such as the resurrection of the dead, the need for the new birth and the deity of Christ. They had come in because of great slackness in the 'transfer' of membership. People could join automatically with a letter of transfer from any Nonconformist church or with the assurance that they had been 'confirmed.' This we decided to deal with painlessly, simply by applying to transfers the same principle that ruled for new converts. That is, they were taught, and then invited to accept what the church stood for. Since very many were being converted, the whole process was introduced quite naturally. No one was expelled, but several people transferred their membership elsewhere, or simply 'left.'

With some members who did not wholeheartedly hold to every detail of our evangelical confession, I was delighted to find fine fellowship and a high level of Christian commitment. The problem was usually one of precise definition, or of bad impressions left long ago by a hard and censorious fundamentalism that confused divine truths with shibboleths. In just a few cases, we proved the truth of Dr Martyn Lloyd-Jones' dictum that if you preach biblical truth with conviction and power, some people simply can't stand it and go away; others who might otherwise have joined never do so.

A firm foundation of faith need not imply witch-hunts and legalism. In a doubtful case we should ask some careful question. What is the *nature* of someone's doctrinal problem? Is he refusing the authority of scripture, or simply expressing an honest difficulty? Is his problem due to the sinful unbelief that is the opposite of faith, or the honest doubting that is a function of faith? Should Job have been put out of church membership? Was it a mistake to keep Thomas in the apostolic band? The answer, I hope, is obvious!

In what *direction* is the person moving? Towards more faith and commitment or *away* from it? Do we require a convert to give assent to a statement of the Trinity defined in fourth-century philosophical terms whose meaning has changed? Or would we accept something like this — 'I am willing to accept everything that the Bible says about God the Father, about Jesus, and about the Holy Spirit. I will not put my own reasoning before difficult statements of Scripture. I will accept the continued teaching of this church on the subject, and try to understand it better'? That is an *attitude* rather than a confession of faith, but it seems a sufficiently good beginning.

A fairly new convert (a very intelligent man) shook me for a moment when he said, 'I won't say I believe the whole Bible, because I haven't *read* the whole Bible.' The first reaction was, 'He doesn't accept the inspiration of scripture.' But in fact he did. He was simply expressing his integrity and acknowledging his ignorance in certain directions. In fact he was perfectly willing to say 'The Bible is God's Word, and I will get to know it as quickly as I can.' He is now a stalwart defender of the faith and a devout Bible student.

FALSE TEACHERS IN PLACES OF POWER

A far bigger problem is created when ministers, theologians and church leaders teach error. Some of the bigger denominations in Britain have systems of promotion which simply ask for this to happen. It is at least arguable that theology as a purely academic exercise is allowable; men with that turn of mind may well study the Bible and produce new ideas about it, as others study Shakespeare, Greek mythology or the Victorian novel. But they should never be confused with Christian teachers (or assumed to be Christians at all, for that matter) simply because their academic discipline is religious. The habit of promoting a theologian sideways, so to speak, so that he suddenly becomes a bishop without adequate parish experience or any proof of a spiritual ministry, can have no possible justification. In Nonconformity the process is curiously reversed, with equally disastrous results. A man has a few years' pastoral ministry in one church, where his theories about secular religion, or a new gospel for a new age, singularly fail to win any secular people or new-age men for Christ, and his church teeters on the verge of closing down. He is then promoted to being lecturer or even principal of a theological college, where he teaches his failure to a whole generation of ordinands. Meanwhile, his last church turns in its need to an evangelical pastor, and changes into a success story. That is no exaggeration; I have seen it happen in every detail.

The major denominations must reconsider the whole relationship between professional theology (whether expressed in research or teaching) and the articles of their faith.

Meanwhile, churches should insist that every college theologian and lecturer *serves at the same time on the pastoral team* of a church. There his ministry can be tested, and his teaching brought under the discipline which every other Christian has to accept.

Quite bluntly there are many theologians whose fundamental personal need is to repent of their unbelief, renounce their flirtation with 'the wisdom of this world', and be converted. In other words, theologians need to be Christians. And church leaders in pastoral care and administration should be drawn exclusively from the ranks of committed Christians of proven faith, whose spiritual ministry is fruitful *before* they are ordained. Until that policy is adopted, our churches will constantly repeat the recurrent scandal of unbelieving leaders who shock or mislead the sheep of Christ's flock, or cause them to stumble.

At the level of theological *training*, the Victorian C.H. Spurgeon's warning continues to be ignored, at great cost. He pointed out that the spiritual and academic equipping of ordinands is a totally different exercise from the training for an academic degree in a secular educational establishment (even in religious subjects). Once a secular degree becomes the aim, the standards, *mores* and philosophical assumptions behind that degree will begin to affect the content of the training. A course of instruction prepared by people who do not know God (even if taught by godly men) gradually shifts the centre of gravity and (to change the metaphor) injects the poison of wordly philosophy into the training of church leaders. In any other sphere, such a policy would be regarded as crazy and self-destructive — as indeed it is.

CONCLUSION

I think the fact has to be faced that tests of orthodoxy and written creeds alone can never safeguard theological purity in the church. Assent to divine truth is ultimately a spiritual exercise, not an academic one. Articles of faith can slow down the advance of error by providing a salient which the orthodox can visibly defend. But only constant renewal in the Holy Spirit can recover the losses made — as every period of revival and reformation displays.

Part Three: The Past

CHAPTER EIGHT

Lessons from History

THE only lesson to be learned from history, avers a cynic, is that nobody ever learns any lessons from history. He has a point. We need to prove him wrong in our case, and take a rapid resumé of how the church has tackled the subject of discipline at various times. I do this with some diffidence. I am no academic historian (as any such person reading this will rapidly discover). I simply pick out a few examples of how some of our forefathers tackled some of our problems. Whether you think they were successful depends on your view of the nature of the church (I am a convinced free-churchman, though, I hope, a tolerant one).

THE EARLY CENTURIES

The early church took Christian behaviour very seriously. Of that there can be no doubt. When the best that bitter critics can do by way of condemnation is to mock and misrepresent virtues, then we can be pretty sure that the virtues existed. Christians were mocked in writing for their sexual purity, kindness to children, strange disinclination to kill baby girls, absence from immoral parties, reluctance to fight, generosity to the poor, good treatment of slaves and healing of the sick. It speaks for itself.

But what happened when they did not come up to standard? A common problem in the second century was 'sin after baptism.' Since no one could possibly expect to be literally *sinless* after baptism, the frequent references to this problem must apply to sins particularly public and grossly inconsistent with a Christian profession. Primarily that meant *adultery* (sexual failure) and *apostasy* (serious abandonment of the faith).

SINS GREAT AND SMALL

There developed a graded classification. Milder sins were dealt with by rebuke, confession and forgiveness (very much in the manner of Matthew 18). 'Deadly sins' led to excommunication. By their nature they did deep harm to the church's community life and public witness. Murder, adultery and perjury brought banishment from membership, whilst apostasy, by definition, was a self-excommunication.

There were sharp differences in the third-century church on the possibility (or otherwise) of restoration after such serious sins. A further tragic sensitive problem was raised by the terrible persecutions which were organised intermittently. These led to scenes of glorious heroism, but not always. What of Christians who just could not endure the imprisonment, interrogation and torture, and denied their faith? As in the earlier discussion, the charitable and positive view prevailed. A distinction was made. Unconverted members who had jumped on the bandwagon in the (quite frequent) times of popularity soon jumped off it again under pressure and threat — and were deemed never to have been truly on it. Those who sincerely desired to follow Christ but simply could not endure torture were welcomed back in better days. It was moving to see how many leaders who pleaded for the 'lenient' view were those who had endured torment themselves for the Name.

Not everyone saw eye-to-eye on these issues. Movements like the Donatists and the Montanists were both (roughly) early examples of puritans and pentecostalists. Their quarrel with the mainline ('Catholic') church was basically about *discipline*; they took the stricter view of what should be expected and what should be done about those who disappointed their expectation.

RIGHT AND WRONG BELIEF

Another problem was about truth and error. Every encounter of the growing church with other cultures and faiths brought the danger of accommodation. (Then, as now, a misguided desire to popularise the gospel by fitting it into the 'spirit of the age' or 'current opinion' could rob that gospel of its very power and introduce heresy.) And every period of rapid church growth brought the danger that semi-pagans would enthusiastically slip into membership, bringing much of their religious error with them. In the third and fourth centuries, four answers were proposed to this problem. *The Scriptures* were gathered and 'canonised' as the inspired Rule of Faith. *Statements of faith* (creeds) were formulated to meet and answer particular errors. Strong *leadership* was developed: especially the office of 'bishop' (originally pastor or elder) was exalted to represent the true faith. Rather later, the idea of 'succession from the apostles' was added to this. In the earliest days that meant, not an automatic handing on of grace, but the evidence that the faith of the apostles was being effectively handed down from generation to generation.

Biblical authority, credal statements and centralised leadership; these were three answers to error. A fourth, more by way of a preventive than an antidote, was *pre-baptismal instruction*. This was taken to ever-increasing lengths. The convert or enquirer's lifestyle, employment and family life were scrutinised. Three years of instruction followed. Finally came a concentrated course led by the bishop himself (the origin of 'Lent', since it preceded the baptisms held annually at Easter). Finally, the baptismal service itself was made into an enormous event, preceded by prayer and fasting, introduced by confession, exorcism and the repeating of the creed, accompanied by impressive ceremonial, and followed by the laying on of hands and first communion.

Augustine, the great African theologian, had an almost scientific approach to *catechising*, as the long instruction was called. (The Greek *katechein* — to instruct, or, literally, to 'keep sounding' appears in seven New Testament references. Luke 1:4 is a suggestive example. It implies face-to-face oral teaching, delivered to an individual or small group, and involving dialogue or discussion.) Augustine advised *catechists* (recognised officers in the church) to get to know the candidates personally and to be careful to treat them as individuals. The starting place should be an enquiry into the candidate's present knowledge or ignorance, motive for learning, and spiritual attitude. This process should continue throughout, 'so that the candidate should be caused to *know*, not only to *hear*.'

The whole thing was a careful and serious attempt to exert discipline both before and after complete Christian commitment. It led to the establishment of the great Catechetical Schools, for example, in Alexandria and Antioch (which in turn became centres for higher education and preparation for church leadership). The advantages are obvious. The disadvantage was that the process made the initial Christian profession something very like a mark of achievement rather than an acceptance of God's grace.

DARK TUNNEL OF THE MIDDLE AGES

The triumph of the papacy was the climax of trends too complex to discuss here. Amongst other things, they totally altered the concept of church discipline. A *sacralist* view prevailed; that is the view of religion and secular government as two sides of one coin. *Inclusivism* is another possible description; the assumption that everyone in a nation or locality (or empire) is a Christian, and that therefore the State and the church are the same thing. (I used to explain rather naughtily to puzzled enquirers the difference between the parish system and the free-church system in these terms. A parish church assumes people to be Christians until they prove that they are not; a free-church system assumes people not to be Christians until they declare that they are. Twenty years ago that might have been a not too unfair description, but in today's pagan British society the parish church is equally a gathering of committed-only.

The inclusive principle prevailed after the Roman empire became 'Christian' — an event which leads many Christians to regard the event as a Fall rather than a triumph, and one almost as cataclysmic as the Fall of Adam. Christianity was certainly spread widely; it was also spread very thin. And because religion and politics were two sides of one coin (probably the very purpose Constantine sincerely had in mind when he declared himself a Christian; the religion of Jesus could provide cement for a crumbling empire) a truly horrific development took place all too quickly. Church leaders saw civic authorities as allies in enforcing both morality and sound theology. Persecuted churchmen became persecuters of heretics.

Sacramentalism was the other development. The ever-increasing confusion of the sign with the thing signified, the symbol with the reality, led to a view of the sacraments (the word originally meant simply a verbal vow) as vehicles of grace. The idea developed of the Christian ministry as a separated and exclusive *priesthood* (nowhere found in this form in the New Testament, where the whole church is the priesthood and Jesus is the great high priest). The sacraments dispensed grace, and the priest dispensed the sacrament. A discipline question about the possibility of a lapsed priest administering sacraments to a lapsed penitent led to a conclusion quite sound *given the starting premise*. God's grace cannot be limited to whether or not a believer *knows* that his priest is a good man, or whether a priest *knows* that the penitent is sincere; it is *God's* grace after all. So it was decreed that grace administered through a sacrament is not dependent upon the state of grace of the people involved. From that point, *ex opere operato* was the inevitable and fatal terminus. A sacrament simply 'works in the working' — that is, the very fact of it being given automatically conveys grace.

SPIRITUAL THREAT AND SECULAR SWORD

Here was a devastating disciplinary weapon. Eternal life (it was believed in the middle ages) depended on reception of the sacraments, especially the mystery of the Mass. The priest had enormous, stunning power. He could simply cut off the supply of grace. A lesser excommunication, therefore, was a banning of the sacrament. The full excommunication was expulsion from the religious body which alone held out any hope of salvation. The treatment could be applied to a person or to a nation. For several years in England, under King John, the nation was placed under an interdict from the pope. National religious and social life came to a standstill. No confession and absolution, no baptism, no communion, no Christian marriage or burial; eternal life was shut off, and the religious life of a nation was in ruins.

On the other hand, civil authorities were seen as allies of the church, and physical penalties could be imposed for irreligious behaviour. Church leaders carefully handed over heretics to the civil authorities and stood by as approving witness to the fining, beating, imprisonment, torture and execution. The almost unbelievable horror of the Inquisition was the end product of a strictly logical route which made a false start.

Now of course as a description of discipline in the medieval Catholic Church, this account is grossly oversimplified. The church performed a remarkable task in lifting the general morality of the 'dark ages,' subduing the barbarism of the pagan invaders who destroyed the Roman empire, and holding peoples together in some kind of order so that civilisation could struggle to life. Protestants can esily forget that there were times under Rome when war was virtually banished between Christian nations, family life was sacred, and the needy were cared for on a vast scale. Moreover, sacraments like penance, confession, Mass and last rites were not by any means always performed mechanically and understood in a materialistic way. Today, 'Renewal Catholics' have also avoided a mechanistic understanding of the sacraments; with an adapted theology and under the influence of a new look at the Bible, many of the sacraments are often being used as vehicles for counselling, healing, evangelical assurance, the pursuit of personal holiness, and parish renewal.

So the whole system of confession and absolution had a great deal of potential for pastoral care, discipline and raising moral standards. Protestants now see what it *became*, and rightly condemn *that* as an intrusion, a mechanical device, and a hindrance to the believer's fellowship with God — not to mention the enormous power it gave to the priesthood. Yet it developed naturally from the thinking of earlier days about serious and less serious sins, the identification of 'deadly sins' and the effort to build a community with standards in which the solemn need for penitence and the joyful assurance of ongoing forgiveness are equally expressed. What went wrong?

First, it tried to apply a legalistic impersonal list of offences to what is essentially a personal spiritual exercise. Second (and arising from that) it prescribed an artificial set of penances — *this* sin requires *this* penance. (I recall a Glaswegian housewife glumly quoting 'I got three Hail Marys and a Glory Be.') Third, it put the pronouncement of penance and forgiveness in the hands of a priesthood, thus changing the whole centre of gravity of the Christian ministry. Fourth, it played down the principle of God's free and gracious pardon, in favour of a system which increasingly gave the impression that *the forgiveness is earned by the penance*. (If it is objected that this was not really taught, then it is a very great pity, and a very great puzzle, that this is exactly what people *thought* they were taught.)

For these reasons the Protestant Reformers said quite rightly that the gospel had got lost in the hierarchy. Hence arose Martin Luther's protest against 'indulgences' (dramatically underlined by the nailing of his famous theses to the church door in Wittenberg, with hammer blows that reverberated around the world). It was not simply a clean-up call against the abuse of the system of indulgences. It sprang from his agonised search for God's forgiveness, his discovery that it flowed freely from the Cross, and his indignation that the very system which had so sedulously taught him that he was a sinner, had carefully hidden the sinners' Saviour from his sight.

Church discipline, then, wandered into a cul-de-sac in the Middle Ages. People who looked for something more obviously related to Jesus and his apostles took refuge in monastic orders. These functioned under the papal umbrella but produced their own 'rules' in which poverty, self-discipline and obedience often reflected the spirit of the Gospels. Others slipped quietly into the ever-present 'medieval underground' of Waldensians, Albigensians, Cathars, Paulicians, Lollards, Hussites and the like. (It is a curious and suggestive fact that in the same period and under very similar circumstances, Francis of Assisi narrowly avoided the displeasure of the pope and thus energised the Franciscans, whilst Peter Waldo narrowly missed the approval of the pope and thus energised the Waldensians, that most persistent and evangelical of medieval 'heresies.') Most of these movements produced strong community discipline, and looked to Matthew 18 as their guide — a fact that was to surface during the Reformation in a striking new way.

REFORMATION TRIUMPH AND TRAGEDY

The Protestant Reformation struck like a whirlwind. The Catholic Church seemed totally unprepared for it, and yet had been moving inexorably towards it. Most of it had been happening for three centuries, but suddenly it convulsed Christendom as if it were a new thing. The Gospel was rediscovered, as the good news of free salvation and new life in Christ. The church was rediscovered as the people of faith, committed to a Gospel which they could not merit but which gripped their lives, demanded their trust and equipped them for obedience. The Bible was rediscovered as the source of truth and the test of all ecclesiastical claims.

But the Reformers inherited the old concept of sacralism, with the impossibilities of discipline which went with it. They continued to see 'church' and 'state' as two sides of one coin. Whole neighbourhoods or nations declared themselves Protestant. Priests became pastors, and continued to serve churches built essentially on the parish system. Members were often a good deal more enthusiastic in rejecting the pope or Rome's political control than in embracing the new birth and justification by faith. If they were truly converted, they found themselves still in membership with many who were not.

Martin Luther toyed with the idea of a separate believers' church, loosely related to the more nominal religious establishment, or even entirely separate from it.

Later he settled for the idea of *ecclesiolae in ecclesia* (a little church of believers within the nominal church — the basis of the 'societies' which later appeared in many state churches). John Calvin admitted that when he first went to Geneva, he found a Gospel, but no church. At first he had some sharp things to say to those who aimed for the impossible ideal of a church of personally committed members.

As soon as it became obvious that the leading Reformers

would stay within the structure and aim to reform it from within, more radical believers parted company with them. The 'Radical Reformation', as it has come to be called, was a dramatic, romantic, tragic page in church history. Catholic and mainline Protestants alike turned in fury on these men who rocked the boat so dangerously by asking for a virtual dismantling of Christendom. Both saw the Radicals as a menace to civilisation. A call for free self-disciplined self-governed assemblies of disciples was seen as a call for the abandonment of law, the destruction of society and the end of religion (rather as the second-century Christians in Rome were regarded as revolutionaries, traitors and irreligious atheists).

The men of the Radical Reformation rediscovered church discipline; it is as simple and radical as that. The main Reformers inherited the idea of civil law enforcing church standards, in a partnership of city and church, nation and religion, empire and Christendom. The earnest discussion about the power of 'the magistrate,' which appears so often in religious writings of the time, is part of this. The magistrate was not a mild Justice of the Peace dispensing fines for driving offences. He was the sword of the state, exercised to enforce its moral and religious standards in the name of the church. So the punishment for Anabaptists (forefathers of modern Baptists) was execution by drowning. A Mennonite (a kind of early Plymouth Brother) could be imprisoned and tortured. Severus was burned at the stake in Geneva as the first modern Unitarian.

To the new Radicals, this was totally abhorrent. That was not simply because it was turned against them, but because it denied their whole New Testament understanding of the church as the freely committed community under the discipline of God. This is important, They did not reject the church-state link because the state persecuted them. Rather, the state persecuted them because they rejected it.

THE GATHERED CHURCH

Matthew 18 stood at the very heart of the Radical Reformation. These 'stepsons of the reformation' were usually called Anabaptists, or Rebaptisers. One of their most controversial beliefs was that infant baptism was invalid. They baptised adult converts only, and 'rebaptised' those who had received that sacrament as children within the Catholic or Protestant churches. But the name is something of a misnomer. Their distinctive stance was *their doctrine of the church.* It could not be disputed by arguments about the absence of any actual mention of child baptism in the New Testament, by assertions that Lydia and the Philippian jailor in Acts 17 must have had children, or by discussions on the parallel of Jewish circumcision. The question was more fundamental. What is the church, and how does it function?

Their favourite expression — 'the rule of Christ' — was in use before they had ever reached any firm conclusions about baptism. They were referring directly to Matthew 18. They looked for a believing community of disciples, with 'Christ in the midst', expressing the certainty of God's forgiveness and applying the adventure of forgiving and helping one another.

Conrad Grebel, the first actually to question infant baptism, did it in these terms. Can a baby consciously belong to a committed fellowship? Can an *adult*, for that matter, unless he is first committed to Christ in personal faith? So — '... even an adult is not to be baptised without Christ's rule of binding and loosing.'

Balthasar Hubmaier, the only pioneer leader allowed to live long enough to draw up a confession of faith and practice, said the same. It came in a *catechism*, significantly.

Question: What is the baptismal pledge?
Answer: It is a commitment which man makes to God publicly and orally before the church...He pledges that he will henceforth set all his faith, hope and trust alone in God, and direct his life according to the divine Word, in the power of Jesus Christ our Lord.... He promises to the church that he desires virtuously to receive from her members and from her fraternal admonition.
Question: But what right has one brother to use this authority on another?
Answer: From the baptismal pledge in which a man subjects himself to the church and all her members according to the word of Christ.

The Reformation tragedy is that the Protestant pioneers like Martin Luther and Ulrich Zwingli found this unacceptable. We can understand and sympathise with their plight, whilst regretting their decision. Gleeful Catholics were saying, 'We told you so! Undermine Mother Church, and you will destroy the fabric of society. Start giving your own interpretation of Scripture and someone else will go a step further and embarrass you as much as you embarrass us.' They accepted the jibe, and reacted against it.

It was certainly not *fear* that made the Reformers hesitate (no one who reads of Luther defying 'the devils in Worms though they be as many as tiles upon the roof-tops,' or of Calvin baring his breast to the swords of the Libertines rather than allow them to defile the Lord's Table, could imagine that). They were simply trapped in the sacralist system. The state must be 'a Christian republic' they insisted. One of them quoted the king of Nineveh in the days of Jonah — he simply commanded the populace to repent and fast. So did Nebuchadnezzar, under Daniel's influence. 'The imperial edict of Nebuchadnezzar teaches all Christian magistrates that they certainly have the prerogative to coerce men to the faith' (Adam Knafft, one of Bucer's leaders).

Any other view (especially little groups of believers presuming to decide for themselves who should be baptised and who should be disciplined) was a direct attack on law and order. 'Let every devout man consider what disruption would ensue,' cried Melanchthon; 'an openly heathen mode of existence would come about.'

So the Reformers proposed 'two marks of a true church' — the word of God 'preached purely,' and the sacraments administered 'according to the institution of Christ.' Maintain *that*, they said, and God will surely work 'amongst the unwieldy mass' of the state church, to produce 'his own little group of true believers, let them be few or many' (agreed at a conference of Protestants).[1]

To this, the Radicals insisted on adding a third mark. The church must act to preserve its faith and its morals. People are either committed to Christ and his church or they are not. If they are, then nurture and discipline are available. If they are not, they should be asked to leave, according to Matthew 18. That was easy enough if the church is a voluntary body. If it is regarded as synonymous with the state, then of course the only way to put someone *out* is to expel him from society — to imprison him, banish him or kill him.

The horrifying irony was that in actual fact the main people to whom 'Christian society' applied its imprisonment, banishment and execution, were the Christians. The whole radical movement was persecuted and hounded almost out of existence.

THE GENEVA EXPERIMENT

Out of the tragic conflict came a synthesis. John Calvin in Geneva established 'that most perfect school of Christ' as Scotland's John Knox described it. He erected a structure and a philosophy of church discipline which merged Reformers' and Radicals' views in a powerfully argued biblical context.

As no city can function without a magistrate and polity, so the church of God needs a spiritual polity. This is however quite distinct from the civil polity, yet does not hinder or threaten it, but rather greatly helps and furthers it.

With a glance over his shoulder, Calvin underlined the difference —

The church does not have the right of the sword to punish or compel ... it is not a question of punishing the sinner against his will, but of the sinner professing his repentance in a voluntary chastisement.

It was back to Matthew 18. The stages of discipline are private admonition, warning in a small group, presentation to the church, and the final extreme of excommunication. The 'keys' are to be used when necessary. He explains, from the context, that the keys of Matthew 16:19 and John 20:22 (given to Peter and then to all the apostles) simply denote the preaching of the gospel. The keys of Matthew 18, however, offered to the whole church mean 'the discipline of excommunication which is entrusted to the church.... The church 'binds' him ... not that it casts him into everlasting ruin and despair, but it condemns his life and morals and warns him of (God's) condemnation. It 'looses' him whom it receives into Communion, for it makes him a sharer of the unity which it has in Christ Jesus.'

At this point Calvin moved towards the Radicals, but stopped halfway. He saw the *elders*, not the whole community of members, as the people who exercised the discipline. *They*, he assumed were the 'witnesses' of verse 15 and the 'church' of verse 16. In other words, the members expressed their will (rather indirectly) through their appointed officers.

What was the purpose of discipline? Calvin put it succinctly. Those who live blatantly unchristian lives must not be regarded as Christians, to the confusion and silencing of the church's witness. The bad must not be allowed to corrupt the good. And finally, those in error mut be shamed or shaken into mending their ways and finding restoration. As an argument for discipline, it has never been bettered.[2]

Notes

1.   For a vivid presentation of this whole story and its implications (including these quotations) see the eminently readable *The Reformers and their Stepchildren* by Leonard Verduin, Exeter, Paternoster, 1965.
2.   Jean Calvin, *Institutes of the Christian Religion*, ed. J.T. McNeill, trans. F.L. Battles, Philadelphia, Westminster Press, 1960, Book II: 'The Discipline of the Church.'

CHAPTER NINE

Pilgrims, Puritans and Preachers

THE lines for church discipline had now been thoroughly laid out. It continued to be a problem for any state-church system, for obvious reasons. Both within and without the national churches, the attempt was made.

PERSECUTED PILGRIMS

In England the principle was seized on by the despised Separatists (Brownists, Barrowists, etc.) who were the pioneers of English Nonconformity. The Church of England was on the horns of that dilemma which is unavoidable when every member of a 'Christian nation' is regarded as a member of the church. The Separatists made the simple, radical assertion that the Christian church is made up of Christians. Only in that way can it possibly preserve Christian purity and exercise Christian discipline. The cost to them was ostracism, derision, social harassment, fines, imprisonment, sometimes execution. The danger they encountered was that of becoming a private cult rather than a universal church. To pursue their vision they abandoned their homes, crossed vast oceans in pitifully small craft, braved hostile savages, built a new home in the wilderness, and established the American nation. *Covenant* was the basic idea. Believers came into a covenant with God, whereby he makes promises to us, we make promises to him, and together, in mutual sympathy and support, Christians work out the implications of both. (A minister friend of mine once claimed that pastoral visitation could normally be kept to fifteen minutes per household, if the pastor went regularly and asked three questions — 'What is God doing for you?' — 'What are you doing for God?' — 'How can I help either of you to do it?' You could certainly call that pastoral care in a nutshell, and it expresses what Separatists were trying to say.)

How did it actually work? There were three types of discipline in a Separatist church. First, there was *care in receiving*. Pastors and elders reported the conversion, character and potential of a new member to the congregation and sought its assent. This involved a good deal more than, 'hands up those in favour.' Browne considered it a lamentable lapse when some churches took the easier way and left it all to the elders. Membership was a matter of mutual commitment.

Second there was *nurture and censure*. As expression of their commitment and involvement (not 'democracy') the members chose their own leaders and entrusted their souls' welfare to them. Pastors encouraged, teachers instructed, elders governed, and deacons organised practical care. Members promised to heed the pastor, learn from the teachers, obey the elders, and give money for the work of the deacons. They also promised to take practical care of each other's Christian growth, and both to give and receive frank advice and warning.

Third, there was *excommunication*. An essential for a New Testament pattern was 'that the church do judge those that are within' in accordance with Matthew 18, and I Corinthians 5. It was the national church's unwillingness (and indeed inability) to do this that brought upon the parish churches the most robust invective from the Separatists. 'Babylon,' 'the False Church,' must be abandoned for this reason, and a profession of conversion was expected to include the element of separation from it (with some well-chosen epithets). No doubt the Separatists went much too far in their abuse, and presented a caricature of the parish church system. But, to them, the very nature of conversion was in dispute. It involved by its very nature, a commitment to a church-disciplined lifestyle. Dead formal religion, on the other hand, was seen not as a failure to know Christ as personal saviour, but a concomitant failure to live in commitment-covenant with Christ's people.[1]

STERN PURITANS

The Puritans carried the torch of serious committed evangelical Christianity *within* the established Church of England. They had to cope with a population which by then gave cheerful assent to anything anti-pope but came a long way short of vital Christian faith and obedience. Yet as followers of Calvin they clung to the concept of a state church. 'In it to win it' might well have been their motto, and their point of departure from the true Separatists.

It was this attempt to take church discipline seriously that earned the astonishment, contempt and derision. They were called 'Puritans' or 'Disciplinarians.' They held to the three marks of a true church (now belatedly accepted in theory by all good Protestants and indeed by many good Catholics!): right preaching of the word, right administration of the sacraments, *and the right exercise of discipline*.

Richard Baxter was a Puritan *par excellence*. His zealous, compassionate, solemn leadership of the parish church in Kidderminster quite literally transformed the whole community. When he began, he could 'hardly find a family that prayed.' When he finished, he could not find a street without its scattering of house-cells. He wielded three weapons: preaching, catechising and discipline. His preaching is what he is frequently remembered for; it had all of Puritanism at its best — biblical, affectionate, powerful, appealing, well illustrated, practical, and profoundly but simply theological. Yet he himself valued the other two exercises even more.

> I study to speak plainly and movingly…. Yet I frequently meet with those who have been my hearers eight or ten years, but know not whether Christ be God or man. Few know the nature of faith, repentance and holiness. I found that half an hour's close personal discourse brought more knowledge and remorse than in ten years of public preaching.[2]

There is the pardonable overstatement of his type here; nevertheless he is saying something vital.

Incidentally, Puritans regarded 'learning the catechism' as a dubious good, if not an actual evil. 'People will learn things by rote and can answer as a parrot, but not understand the thing.' Not rote answers but dialogue and discussion was the purpose. 'Learning the words and syllables rather than the great things of God will leave them neither wiser nor better,' warned Issac Watts.

Through two successive ministries I have experimented with something very like Baxter's 'close discussion,' on a voluntary basis, after finishing an evangelistic or doctrinal sermon with the offer of 'home instruction' for those who were moved. In small groups of three or four we have then worked through basic principles of Christian belief and behaviour. I have seen a whole group decide that the Bible standards of sexual morality, family principles etc., were too high for them, and take church membership no further after the three-month course. Thus false and superficial professions of conversion have been avoided. But many others, numbering several hundred, have been ready for baptism and church membership when the course was over — and have then moved on to a membership preparation class, and after that a nurture group. We used various names — Baptismal Class, Enquirers Class, Discipleship Class, Christian Basics, etc., and the atmosphere and direction varied a good deal. The leader need not be the pastor, and sometimes the church had three or four groups running concurrently. It was an unintended reflection of Baxter's method, but without his strong paternalism and authoritarianism.

Catechisms were not invented by the Puritans, as we have seen. But Puritans immensely increased the use of them. Baxter could speak of 'hundreds' of catechisms in use, each the slightly varying product of an individual pastor. Not to be outdone, the successors to the Scottish Covenanters required stern spot checks on ministers at irregular but frequent intervals, to ensure that they took catechising seriously. A black-mark system, not unlike the endorsements on a modern driving licence, followed ministerial slackness in this respect — admonition for the first failure, rebuke for the second, and dismissal for the third.

So much for Richard Baxter's second weapon (preaching was the first). Together, they ensured understanding and application of the faith, and a personal dealing with the people's souls. It was termed *preventative discipline*, and its value for today's church is obvious.

His third weapon (and that of all Puritans) was *corrective discipline*. The Westminster Confession provided for it. Once more, it is based on Matthew 18. An offender was to be 'admonished privately' (by pastor and elders). If he persisted, he was to be 'admonished publicly' — presumably his name and offence was mentioned from the pulpit. If this in turn had no effect, the 'lesser excommunication' took place. This meant temporary exclusion from the Communion Table. When even this had no effect, the 'greater excommunication' (ejection from membership) took place. The incident of the Corinthian offender (I Corinthians 5:4) was regarded as in a sense handing the offender over to the tender mercies of Satan, who would have every opportunity to stir up distress of soul and pangs of conscience without any assurance of pardon. Notice, the hapless offender is still assumed to *have* a conscience! Basically, he is seen as a Christian in disobedience, not an unfeeling outsider. Restoration is the end in view. This was the method employed during the Commonwealth period, under Cromwell's elastic but evangelical concept of a

'Free' state church.

We may smile today (or wince) at some of the reasons given for rebuke and warning. But these people were deadly serious. Flagrant sins like immorality or theft were given just one offer of restoration, which if rejected led to swift expulsion. By their very nature, such acts were public and caused public scandal.

CAUSES FOR DISCIPLINE

Neglect of corporate worship was regarded very seriously. A 'oncer' would not have been regarded as a serious member in the first place. Public worship, communion, midweek prayers, these were the minimum expectation.

Preference for the company of unbelievers was frowned on and rebuked — especially if it led to romantic ties or to marriage. Thomas Brooks, with his usual way with words, says (in seeking a life partner) 'look more for a portion of grace than a portion of gold, more after righteousness than riches, more at inheritance in heaven than on earth, more at being new-born than high-born'.[3]

Strangely to us, 'worldliness of dress' was considered to be a red light flashing. To be up with the fashion was scarcely a sign of high value placed on the company of God's people. One recalls the reasons why John Bunyan's Pilgrim and Faithful caused such offence in Vanity Fair; they would not dress like the citizens, would not talk like them and would not buy their wares.

REPENTANCE AND RESTORATION

Now all this may seem harsh and severe to us. Certainly some of it opened a door to externalism, pharisaism and a narrow cribbing view of life. It invited the cutting comment of Carlyle that Puritans opposed bear-baiting, not because of the pain it gave the bear, but because of the pleasure it gave the onlookers. But in general, this discipline was exercised with care, conscientousness and deep spirituality. The growing millions of people hurt and scarred by the outworking of permissiveness today would have been less hurt by Puritan sternness. Discipline was not applied 'hastily or frivolously' as John Owen says. Baxter would call for three days fasting and prayer in the congregation before taking the final step. Tears were frequent and genuine amongst those passing judgement. Even at this stage *restoration* was still the main purpose; 'corrective not vindictive, for healing not for destruction' was Owen's dictum. The sorrowing congregation was reminded of its own liability to stumble, and warned against censorious self-righteousness.

Nor was the talk of restoration merely formal and dutiful. Restoration services were regular too. Private counsel and hopeful evidence of penitence led to a service of prayer and praise, public confession only if the offence had been specially public, and the laying on of hands for the restored member.

Such was Puritan discipline. Baxter argued that it was an essential, without which the Gospel could not prosper.

> If ministers would be conscientious in performing this duty ... they might make something of it and expect a blessing from it. But when we shrink from all that is dangerous and ungrateful in our work, and shift of all that is costly or troublesome, we cannot expect that any great good will be effected ... we cannot look that the gospel should run and be glorified.'[4]

THE MEN WHO SET BRITAIN ALIGHT

The eighteenth century in Britain and America saw that amazing phenomenon, the Great Awakening. Multitudes of people were swept into vital Christian living, and streams of social and moral healing released that pioneered almost everything decent and just in our modern societies. Wesleyan Methodism was one result. What marked Wesleyanism above all else was the commitment to *discipline in community*. A close student of the scene has suggested that there is no parallel in the modern church, and that the normal commitment to Christian community of an eighteenth-century Methodist 'would be regarded as incredible by almost all members of any Christian communion (in America) today'.[5]

How did it work? The *class* was the cornerstone of the structure. Its purpose was not teaching (as the name might suggest) but mutual help and encouragement in very small groups. A class met for one hour each week. Members shared any good experiences or unfortunate failures of the week. (As it was all done in sixty minutes, this could not have been at the interminable length of lugubrious soul searching that we might imagine, and which we sometimes suffer in modern housegroups!) Members discussed what went wrong (or right), shared advice and encouragement, prayed for each other. They each contributed one penny which went into a central stewards' fund for the help of the poorest members and the support of the unpaid travelling preachers.

All of this was begun prior to acceptance into 'membership'.

With mental visions of the vast crowds which gathered to hear the open-air evangelists and the dramatic results attendant on their preaching, it is a surprise to discover that *most of the conversions actually occurred in the class meeting*. Wesley and Whitefield normally only 'counselled' the few who came under immediate physical and emotional distress in the mass meetings. Other people would thrust scribbled notes into their hands expressing interest or conviction. But the general conclusion to a great evangelistic appeal was: (*a*) Get alone with God and seek the Saviour. (*b*) Start meeting with Christians in a small group and learn what Christian life and faith mean. (This is not unlike the method adopted by Billy Graham and the organisers of Mission England in 1984. Although there were 'open appeals,' the sheer numbers involved often made the counsellors' task little more than gathering personal details so that the enquirer could be firmly guided into a 'nurture group.' Within a few weeks, in my area, we were seeing enquirers both from the mission and also some who had appeared since the mission, coming to faith within the nurture groups.)

Howard Snyder goes so far as to claim that there never was one continuous wave of revival lapping over the country. Rather, as the preachers restlessly quartered the country on horseback, preaching in city squares and on village greens, localised 'revivals' sprang up, only spread and interconnected by the class meetings. Without *them*, 'the scattered fires of renewal would have burned out long before the movement was able to make a deep impact.'[6]

HOW THE CLASS WORKED

Within the class there was discipline as well as discipling. Each member carried a ticket signed by that benevolent dictator John Wesley himself. This ticket could be withheld or withdrawn for unsatisfactory behaviour, lapsing into drunkenness, dubious friendships etc. The class leader kept a sharp eye on weekly progress (or lack of it). Wesley's occasional visits as he beat a regular path between London, Bristol and Newcastle, were as much for 'regulating the classes' as for repeat evangelistic preaching. As many as a quarter of the members might not survive his examinations and purges, as he called them. Loss of a ticket meant debarrment from the quarterly love-feast, at which celebration, worship, teaching and communion were all conducted in an atmosphere which we would call warmly charismatic.

A check of any edition or digest of Wesley's diary reveals how much the discipline was needed, and how badly converts could fall. Drunkenness, smuggling, violence, swearing, lying, stealing, were all firmly dealt with. At the class level, the faults were not doctrinal or even particularly religious, but social, to do with getting on with your neighbour. Wesley was building a community, not a religious club.

BAND AND SOCIETY

There were two more layers to the Methodist system. The band was what we might call the midweek meeting (though not as we see it an optional extra). The band member never missed a week 'without some extraordinary reason.' This was a kind of spiritual health-check, more specifically religious than the class. Unlike the class, it was for committed Christians only and majored on exhortation, teaching, and (something that got it into a great deal of trouble with critics) open confession. Snyder estimates, surprisingly, that only about one Methodist in five joined a band. Even more surprising to us is the organisation of two more regular groups — the Select Society for those showing unusual ability, promise or seriousness (a kind of spiritual advanced drivers' course) and the Penitents, who had been disciplined, or felt they were slipping, but still seem to have been perfectly willing to attend.

Finally, the whole system of classes, bands and other groups, was bound together in a society. This at first was a section of the local parish church (something like Luther's *Ecclesiolae in Ecclesia* made up of those who were really serious about Christianity. Later, when the open break came with Anglicanism, the society became in name what it already was, a local evangelical church: a Methodist Church, in fact.

This was the earnest, warm, disciplined church-commitment of the Awakening which did as much for the moral and social transformation of the English-speaking nations as did the tremendous evangelistic preaching. In an excess of humility, George Whitefield congratulated Wesley on its achievement, and claimed that his own converts in contrast had been 'formed into a rope of sand'. This was scarcely true, as most of Whitefield's converts (being Calvinistic rather than Arminian) joined the Presbyterians or the Baptists, or became loyal members of the Evangelical wing of the Established Church. There they may not have encountered precisely the organising genius of Wesley, but the 'societies' of the Anglican Church, the 'experience meeting' of the Welsh Calvinistic Methodists, the 'catechising classes' of Presbyterianism and the 'bands' of the Moravians provided something fundamentally similar. The still continuing 'East Africa Revival' and the 1984 Mission England are both topical examples of the effective and indeed essential role of the class system in modern church life.

A COMMON PATTERN

It is time to sum up the lessons of history. The church has only been strong when it has taken discipline seriously. The pattern has repeated itself. Care in defining Christian commitment as both vertical and horizontal led to care in evangelising, catechising and preparation for membership. The life of discipleship was nurtured and guarded by small-group fellowship involving sharing, caring and rebuking. Multiple lay leadership worked hand in hand with ordained clergy. Expulsion from the fellowship was a serious last resort.

Notes

1. Alan Tovey, 'Adding to the Church — in the Teaching of the Elizabethan Separatists' in Papers given at the Westminster Conference, 1973, pp20–30.
2. Richard Baxter, *Reformed Pastor* (London, 1656), quoted in 'Discipline in the Puritan Congregation,' *Puritan and Reformed Studies Conference*, London, Tyndale, 1959, pp30–37.
3. Denis Downham, 'Discipline in the Puritan Congregation' in *Puritan and Reformed Studies Conference*.
4. Ibid.
5. Howard Snyder, *The Radical Wesley*, IVP, 1980, p54.
6. Ibid., p57.

CHAPTER TEN

House Church — High Road or Cul-de-sac?

CHARISMATIC renewal is perhaps the most widespread and colourful feature in modern church life. 'Restoration' is an offspring of that renewal. Restoration churches are even more radical than renewal churches. They blame the formalism, complacency and traditionalism into which previous revival movements have eventually fallen, on some fundamental fault in the basic structure. Jesus' warning (about old wineskins which cannot contain effervescent new wine) is often quoted. One-man clergy and pseudo-democracy — with church affairs managed by committees — are seen as the basic causes of renewal lapse.

The 'household churches' (as they are often called) offer a striking alternative. Powerful charismatic leadership, small-group fellowship, lay leadership offering informal teaching; unstructured worship in which all take part; derision of everything traditional and structured — these are some of the features of the alternative offered. In course of time, the inevitable has happened. After a short spell marked by a cheerful free-for-all, unordained leaders have developed large fellowships, and house fellowships have grown as big as large churches. A new clergy and a new denomination have arrived — or rather, several different denominations with their characteristic emphases, magazines, celebration events, and leadership structures.

The distinctive feature of the house church has now emerged. It is *discipline*. Church membership is seen as entry to an army barracks, not a hospital. Tiered layers of leadership provide the key to nurture, growth, control and guidance.

And the horror stories have begun. People have nervous breakdowns because of pressure put on them to conform. Marriage engagements are broken off when leaders forbid them. Families have to subject their household accounts to elders. People are refused permission to change jobs or move house.

Members become zombies who lose the ability to make their own decisions. Crazy schemes are pronounced as prophecies, and hesitation to follow them is denounced as arguing with God. People come back to traditional or charismatic churches emotionally bruised and scarred — or they slide back into non-Christian living.

House church leaders indignantly deny the charges. Renegades always have to justify themselves, they say. Well, yes, they admit, perhaps there have been some excesses, but the answer to abuse is not disuse but right use. A new work of God can always expect the special attention of Satan, the accuser of the brethren. Traditonal degree-oriented clergy are jealous of the success of their lay rivals, and exaggerate the faults. In a splendid piece of jargon-rhetoric, one writer tells us:

> Dynamite is dangerous. Fearing the danger, some prefer to chip marble from the quarry with hammer and chisel — much safer, but impossibly slow. Far better to use dynamite *wisely and responsibly* to blast out tons of rock in a matter of minutes. Authority is dangerous too. Some prefer to play safe and snipe at Satan's citadel through democratic or anarchical pea-shooters. All they'll produce is pea-plants growing round the walls. Far better to be a kingdom people, a people at home with true spiritual authority, and thus blast holes in the satanic defences for King Jesus!'

Well — what is the truth of it? Has this movement recalled the church to New Testament principles of authority and discipline? Has it shown us the high road? Or does it beckon us into a cul-de-sac with a quagmire at the other end? Now of course it is rash and unfair to generalise about a whole diverse movement (whether for or against). But we need to ask two questions as we look at the house church movement. First — what is the Holy Spirit saying that needs to be heard? Second — what are its mistakes which need to be heeded?

Look at the positive contribution. The movement reminds us of things which have been forgotten by the traditional churches — and perhaps were sometimes never even there to forget in the first place. *It is concerned to make disciples, not just converts.* So is the Bible. A quick check with a Bible concordance is enough to establish that for every use of words like 'converted,' 'born again' and 'forgiven,' there are a dozen examples of the word 'disciple.' The foundation command for the church (its marching orders as the militaristic Duke of Wellington called it) is to make disciples, to baptise and to teach the disciples to do everything that Jesus commanded (Matthew 28:19). It rests on Christ's kingly authority (verse 18). Much of the structure of the house churches is designed to do precisely that.

Secondly the movement sees *the horizontal relationship as being an essential part of the vertical*. So does the Bible. A Christian without a deep church commitment is a contradiction in terms. The *koinonia* — the fellowship — is not simply a useful follow-up agency for converts who make a personal decision to put their faith in Christ, perhaps in some great evangelistic crusade or local mission. To come into fellowship with God in Christ is to come into the body of Christ, the church, the kingdom. A convert is not a baby who suddenly comes to birth in an empty field, but hears that nearby are supplies of milk (the Bible), a public telephone box (prayer) and some motherly folk fairly willing to offer nurture (the church). No — the new convert is born again by the Spirit of God, given new life and identity which carries with it as an essential part of its very existence an appetite for God's word, a desire to pray, and *a place in the family*. The house church movement gives immense emphasis to this, but no more than the New Testament itself does. Its leaders are deeply concerned to build a network of training, pastoral care and mutual commitment at every level of practical need and in every area of discipleship growth. 'Spell it out and God will do it', seems to be their motto. 'Pin it down, and serious Christians will see it, want it, and beg for it.'

Thirdly, the movement explores, further than most, that profoundest of New Testament symbols of the church — *the Body of Christ*. Blinkered thinking or limited commitment so often brings disease to the church and stunts its growth. Limbs may suffer from *atrophy* as they fail to receive nourishment, from *paralysis* because they never exercise themselves, from *cancer* as they enlarge at the expense of every other limb. Some bodies are afflicted with *palsy* as every limb jerks into independent action. Some bodies suffer *arthritis*: the joints between the members don't function. *Asthma* afflicts some; inspiration is almost non-existent.

My Baptist forefather Charles Spurgeon gently jeered at the Plymouth Brethren for 'teaching that every part of the body should be a mouth.' His denominational descendants have certainly not slipped into that mistake, but we often seem to imagine that the biggest part of the body is designed to sit on committees.

The apostle Paul, of course, indulges in similar mild humour as he pictures a body in which the foot gets depressed because it can't hold a pen, and the ear gets an inferiority complex because it can't see very well. Just as foolish is a proud eye which despises the feet because they are colour-blind, or a beautiful face which feels that the sex organs have no importance because they are kept covered (I Corinthians 12:14–24). 'All of you are Christ's body, and each one is a part of it' (verse 27). The charismatic renewal has done much to restore that reality in so far as it affects and implements the working of spiritual gifts and abilities and offices within the church. This is what Paul first does in this chapter, with his talk of wisdom and knowledge, of conquering faith and healing ministry, of prophecy and of tongues (verses 4–11). The house church movement has gone further, and insisted that a biblical structure of leadership and mutual care is needed, if the gifts are ever to be employed properly. That is exactly what Paul goes on to say too.

> If one part of the body suffers, all the other parts suffer with it; if one part is praised, all the other parts share its happiness...In the church God has put all in place.'
>
> I Corinthians 12:26, 28

Fourthly, the movement has an emphasis on *godly order and authority*. This is in stark contrast to the permissiveness, chaotic disorder and lunatic expressions of liberalism and democracy which are so much a feature of today's world inside and outside the church. So does the Bible. Whatever mistakes and excesses there may have been in the movement (and honesty will compel us to examine them soon) it stands four-square where the great majority of God's saints have stood until about a hundred years ago, and where every scripture writer tells us to stand. *God rules* in wisdom, love and power. The universe, in its unfallen state, was an ordered universe with every species of animal and plant 'after his kind' as the AV used to say (Genesis 1:12) with every star possessing its 'own glory' (I Corinthians 15:41), with every angel in its right 'estate' (Jude 6).

That order is part of the orderliness of a God-ordered creation. Only because a great deal of it still survives (even in a fallen world) can the universe continue to exist and make any sense. Water does not run downhill on Mondays and uphill on Tuesdays. The sun does not rise in the East in summer and the West in winter. The predictability of nature is part of nature's order and a product of God's orders. That alone makes science possible, incidentally.

All of this is part of the Christian doctrine of creation. The doctrine of sin tells us that first Satan and then Adam resisted that order and rebelled against that authority. There were angels who 'did not stay within the limits of their proper authority' (Jude 6). There was a man and a woman who resented God when he said, 'This is off-limits' (Genesis 3:1–7). The dire result was that mankind, rebelling against his proper place in the hierarchy, lost the very authority which God had given him.

> You appointed him ruler over everything you made;
> You placed him over all creation.
>
> Psalm 8:6

But he muffed it, as we say in the north of England. He spoiled it and lost it by stepping out of line. 'We do not see man ruling over all things now. But we do see Jesus' — the only example of man as he should be, perfectly occupying his place in the hierarchy, 'crowned with glory and honour' (Hebrews 2:5–9) and heading up in turn that new humanity, the Church, which delights to take its proper place again in the divine scheme of things, under God's order and authority.

The house church movement unashamedly takes that position. It does not allow Women's Lib to panic it into jettisoning the place of woman, wife and mother, in God's order for family and church. It does not allow democratic liberalism with a religious face to invade the church meeting or the parochial church council. Equality, though a deeply significant word in political thinking and economic relationships, becomes almost meaningless when applied to spiritual realities. Clearly no one can be 'equal with God' (it was Adam's sin to imagine he could be). Nor can we talk about 'rights' in relationship to the creator on whose constant outflow of life and energy we depend for our existence. 'Who are you, my friend, to answer God back? A clay pot does not ask the man who made it, "Why did you make me like this?"' (Romans 9:20). The closest we may get to equality is to say that we are equally loved by God (though I am not at all sure that the Bible says even that). However, that certainly does not mean that we have a 'right' to be loved by God, since his love is totally sovereign, gracious, and unrelated to anything that we are or deserve. Moses could get no further than saying God loves you because he loves you (Deuteronomy 7:7–8).

Certainly, 'all people are equal' is a statement which means less the more we examine it. Are we equally good-looking? Clearly not. Equally clever? Hardly. Equally fortunate? Certainly not. Do we have equal abilities? No one imagines so. Do we occupy equal positions, perform equally important jobs or have equal needs? It would be hard to argue that we do. A works manager and a tea boy do not have equal positions; an electricity power worker and an ice-cream vendor do not perform equally important jobs; a newborn baby and a seventy-year-old do not have equal needs. The positions within a family, of a bread-winning father, retired grandfather, nursing mother, working son, schoolgirl daughter and visiting aunty, are clearly neither the same nor equal. A teacher and a pupil are not equal in either knowledge or authority; if they were, they would cease to be teacher and taught, for either the teacher would have nothing to teach or the pupil would need nothing to learn.

Of course 'order' can be corrupted, and often is. A man may bully his wife and drive his children to despair. The Bible recognises this, and forbids it. An employer may ill-treat his employees, and a governor may prove unfit to govern. The Bible recognises that too. A church leader may 'love to have the pre-eminence' (3 John 9, AV) and earn rebuke for doing so. But none of this alters the fact that God wills order, and expresses that will in a man's rule over his household, an employer's responsibility to his staff, a government's duty to rule and a church leader's authority to teach and guide.

Bible scholars are fairly widely agreed that a regular pattern of such teaching is found in the New Testament, and represents a kind of primitive practical catechism taught to those who committed themselves to Christian living.

> Submit yourselves to one another *because of your reverence for Christ*. Wives, submit to your husbands *as to the Lord*.... Husbands, love your wives *just as Christ loved the church*.... Children, it is your Christian duty to obey your parents.... Parents, do not treat your children in such a way as to make them angry.... Slaves, obey your human masters ... *as though you were serving Christ*.... Masters, behave in the same way.
>
> Ephesians 5:21—6:9

The Epistle to the Romans contains a similar section, and includes the matter of obedience to the state as well, 'because no authority exists without God's permission, and the existing authorities have been put there by God' (Romans 13:1).

Peter's version is remarkably similar, too (1 Peter 3:1–7). The writer to the Hebrews particularly specifies the authority of church leaders; 'remember' them, 'imitate their faith,' 'obey them and follow their orders' is the pattern — because 'they watch over your souls without resting, since they must give God an account of their service' (Hebrews 13:7, 17). It is a passage of which George Whitefield said it 'shook my soul like an earthquake'.

Now it is precisely this divine order which the house church movement tries to come to grips with. It is the basis of two of the movement's most distinctive teachings. The Christian household is seen as an essential unit in discipleship, with the father/husband acting as priest, responsible for and 'covering' the family. His failure to take that responsibility, or the refusal of wife and children to accept it, are regarded as prime reasons for discipleship breakdown, lack of answer to prayer, and spiritual ill-health in the church.

Secondly, the house churches erect hierarchical structures, differing in detail, but variously involving household groups, neighbourhood groups, group leaders or shepherds, joint elderships, and inter-church authority from 'prophets' or 'apostles.' These function on what is called (by some friends and many critics) the 'pyramid pattern.' Families are guided by leaders, leaders by elders and pastors, elders and pastors by prophets and apostles. Women are not seen as potential leaders, pastors are not seen as one-man ministers, and there is no 'head' of the pyramid (as one might logically expect) because pastors and apostles are seen as mutually 'covering' one another.

It is these last features which cause most adverse comment, and around these the horror stories most often circulate. But let us first acknowledge that the movement is here dealing with a profound and fundamental scriptural truth. In coming to grips with authority, order and hierarchy it is not unique, nor as novel as either it or its critics seem to think. Most Christian movements of the past have wrestled with them. We have already seen that in an earlier chapter.

Authority, order and rule are fundamental laws of creation. Acceptance of them should be a matter of common sense, for there are parables of it in everyday life. I recall the eager Nigerian in the last days of colonialism, who said ecstatically, 'Independence means that we will be able to drive on any side of the road we like!' But of course they couldn't. A sport without rules is unthinkable and unworkable. So is a nation without laws, a society without regulations, a family without order, a club without rules or a church without authority. But it is more than a matter of common sense. Repentance and faith in Jesus Christ involve a willing restoration of God's rules, a heart that loves his commandments and enrolment in a church that expresses his will, in order and authority. What does the Kingdom of God mean, if not that?

Arthur Wallis in a sensitive and perceptive article discusses this:

> In churches where New Testament principles are applied, one would expect that major decisions such as a couple becoming engaged, changing jobs, moving house out of the area, and *all decisions which affect others in the church* would be referred as a matter of course to the elders for their prayerful consideration and counsel. It is not a question of doing this under duress. In fact most people, especially young couples, are most grateful for such counsel, for they know it may save them from blunders which they have seen others making.[2]

Confronting One Another. Notice the wording in particular here, for it is exactly the kind of thing which raises hackles amongst those who fear a tyrannical eldership. Moreover, it is the basis for many of the horror stories which, uncomfortably often, prove to be true. But notice the phraseology. 'One would expect' ... 'decisions which affect others' ... 'referred for prayerful consideration and counsel' ... 'most grateful for such counsel.' Kept within these terms, the approach is not only commendable, but, with slightly different wording and in marginally different contexts, it is often adopted in 'traditional' churches. In fact, if one replaced 'elders' with 'pastor' or 'minister,' it is a fair description of the kind of thing which not only fills a traditional minister's life but overworks and crushes him because people want him to carry it all alone, without a shared eldership.

Both with and without a supporting and sharing eldership, my role as a Baptist pastor has brought to me every one of the examples quoted. Often.

Becoming engaged? A good pastor and youth leader will often see it happening before the couple concerned see it — and if either has any serious sense of responsibility will often have quite strong views on their suitability or otherwise. Almost certainly the couple will come immediately to share the news and to seek advice and counsel about Christian marriage. Why not come *before* the decision is made, if they really want advice? I recall a case in which the girl was not a committed Christian. At my advice the engagement was cancelled. This shook the girl so hard she was converted. They then became engaged again, married, went to the mission field, and twenty years later introduced me to their three daughters who all keenly served the Lord.

In my most recent pastorate, where the church became a fast-growing family fellowship, we had to face the implications of early marriage and the horrifying divorce statistics that go with it. Marriage preparation became too frequent a task for the pastor alone. A care-and-counsel group which already functioned in the church offered to take on the task. The group was made up of quite skilled people (doctors, doctors' wives, social workers and experienced counsellors) who had accepted training for general case work. They produced a first-class course of marriage preparation which covered such things as compatibility, finance, sexual morality, family principles and God's order in the home. The elders agreed to 'strongly suggest' acceptance of the course to all who asked for marriage in the church. I think, on reflection, that we should have made it tougher — *a condition* of being married in church (as the counselling group in fact wanted us to do). After all, what sense or rightness is there in a couple saying (in effect) 'we want this church to marry us, but we are not prepared to listen to this church's understanding of what marriage is'?

Arthur Wallis's other examples are much the same. *Changing jobs?* How many pastors have written out character references on request, and how many expect to discuss with the applicant his hopes and plans, his suitability and his motives? A character reference is a serious thing, and no minister worthy of his calling sees himself as churning them out *automatically*, like the signing of passport applications. Next to the God he chooses and the woman he marries, a man makes no more far-reaching decision than that of his employment. Not only the pastor but the eldership (or diaconate, or pastoral team) will often discuss the wisdom or otherwise of a member's change of job.

Moving house out of the area? Here is another decision fraught with great consequence. How often pastoral leaders deplore a 'move out' for unconvincing reasons which leaves a vital church task unfulfilled. How often we regret to see a family decide on a house, buy it, and *then* start asking 'Is there a live, sound church anywhere near for ourselves and our children?'

Arthur Wallis rebuts ideas of an eldership involving interference, coercion and tyranny over minute details of private life like buying a hi-fi, boy-girl friendships, domestic budgeting, etc. He says,

> A wise shepherd will sometimes refuse to bring any word of positive *direction*, but simply a word of *advice*, which the believer must weigh and then come to his own decision....

> Notice how Paul sometimes gave his judgement rather than a
> definite injunction (I Corinthians 7:25).

This is well said.

What categories should in fact come under pastoral advice and
guidance? He proposes:

> every area of your life which affects
> — your fellowship with God
> — your walk and behaviour as a Christian
> — your function in the church
> — your witness before the world.

It is a thought-provoking list. He is *simply taking Christian commitment, discipleship and church membership seriously*. A Christian who does not wish to have such areas scrutinised and commented on by fellow Christians is not taking fellowship very seriously at all. Church leaders who shrink from getting entangled in
such areas of their members' lives should perhaps think again
about their call to leadership. Churches of the democratic
church-meeting type of government are rightly concerned at the
danger of the membership losing its voice to the power of a few
élitist elders. However, they should look at their own history.
This is how the church meeting functioned in the past, when its
principles were first enunciated. I dipped into a hundred-year-
old minute book from my Baptist Church in the north of England, and found the Church Meeting discussing and approving
the exclusion of members for the following reasons:

> Denying the divinity of Christ ... intoxication ... receiving the
> amorous addresses of an unbeliever ... disorderly conduct,
> lying and deceit ... showing a degree of obstinacy when
> rebuked for not speaking according to the law and testimony
> ... contention and disharmony and contempt of the pastor.

Clearly, these matters were brought before the church by leaders
who had been handling them for some time. Several reports
included the phrase, 'after twice being admonished.' It seems to
have been not unlike a modern game of football — two warnings,
and the third time the player was sent off!

The theory of the house church movement, then, *seems* to be
based on a thoroughly biblical view of church membership commitment on the one hand and leadership responsibility on the
other. Moreover, it is not really new. The spiritual ancestors of

many of our traditional churches pursued the same goals. The discipline of the Mennonites, the 'little church within a church' of the Lutherans, the 'societies' of eighteenth-century Anglicanism, the class meeting of early Methodism, the experience meeting of Welsh Calvinistic Methodism; all are examples of the same vision. In that respect, the house churches remind us of our roots and recall us from our carelessness. Why, then, do so many Christians fear that they have taken a wrong turning? That question requires another chapter.

Notes

1. Editorial in *Restoration* (May 1984).
2. Arthur Wallis, 'Confronting one another' in *Restoration* (May 1984), pp31–34.

CHAPTER ELEVEN

Warning Signs

IN the style of C.S. Lewis's *Screwtape Letters*, a friend of mine suggested that the demon who invented the scare-phrase 'pyramid movement' earned an immediate rise, and the demon who linked the words 'authority' with the word 'cult' featured in Satan's next honours list. He may be right. But if so, those shady figures found plenty of ready material available to promote their propaganda.

Perhaps we should dismiss nine-tenths of the shocking stories about the house church. Some of them deserve to be dismissed. They have already become established evangelical apocrypha.

What is left? Quite enough to be disturbing. I know some of them personally to be true. What is the cause? The inevitable blemishes inherent in any new movement staffed by human beings? Or some fundamental flaw in the basic philosophy?

A FATAL FLAW?

So far I have quoted house church principles from one respected high quality magazine.

Rather different, however, is a small book lent to me by another friend. He belongs to a little church bravely determined to get back to its roots and to adopt New Testament principles of church-building. 'What did I think of this particular approach?' he asked. It looked good, and yet, somehow…? I soon found the reason for my reservations and his. In one shattering sentence it takes the reader from unarguable truth to highly dangerous error. It can easily happen.

I want to be totally fair, so I shall carefully quote the writer. This care is needed because the flaw in its logic is truly horrendous, but appears so innocent. One wants to be quite sure that he has really said it — and one wishes that he had not. And of course he can only be held to represent his own immediate circle.

He begins rightly with a vital principle — the command of Jesus to *make disciples*, baptising them and teaching them to observe (NIV 'obey') all that he commanded (Matthew 28:18–20). The principle is disciples not converts; obedience not mere belief; and authority vested in Jesus. The picture he is drawing is that of a community of such disciples who could appropriately be called a body, a kingdom, a family, a church. True.

'So only disciples enter,' he continues. 'How do they get in? Through what door?'

Jesus gives the answer, he tell us, in John 10, which he quotes in part as, 'I am the door of the sheep ... he who does not enter by the door into the fold of the sheep, but climbs up some other way, he is a thief and a robber.'

So Jesus is the door. Immaculate reasoning. The whole context of John 10 is that of discipleship, salvation, and entering the fold.

But now comes the chilling leap — truly a leap into the dark, in its implications.

> As Jesus is now not physically on the earth, his body and espe-
> cially its leaders, replace him in this function.... In a restora-
> tion church the elders or the leaders, in plurality, are 'the door
> of the fold'.[1]

Stop there. It is so easy to hurry past one sentence, but that sentence is dynamite.

First, there is a mixing of metaphors, which is not conducive to clear thinking. 'Jesus is the door. But as the Church is the body of Christ, its leaders become the door in his place.' Switching images from door-and-sheepfold to body-and-members halfway through a statement lands us in confusion. The fact that Jesus is the door has nothing to do with his physical presence or absence in the world. It is to do with the access to the Father that he has obtained for us, the salvation he wrought for us at the cost of his own life and the liberty within the church (flock and fold) which he give to us because of our relationship with him. Read the whole allegory as Jesus gives it in John 10 and that is obvious. On the other hand the metaphor of the church as the body of Christ *is* to do with the Saviour's physical absence from the world. It is also to do with the expression of Christ's will and work through the church, and the interrelationship of Christians within the church.

Second, there is a misunderstanding. The 'body of Christ' is a rich metaphor and a glorious spiritual reality. It is, as all agree, one consequence of Christ's physical absence, *but it has nothing to do with his 'replacement.'* 'His body, and especially its leaders, *replace him,*' says our writer. But to replace Christ is unthinkable. He is unique and unchanging, 'the same yesterday, today and forever.' In the New Testament the name Antichrist is given precisely to that which seeks to replace Christ, or take his place (I John 2:18). Unfortunately the Good News Bible here renders 'Antichrist' as 'Enemy of Christ.' Whilst that is true, the sense of the Greek is not so much 'opposing Christ' as 'supplanting or replacing Christ.' Westcott suggests, 'someone who assails Christ by proposing to do or to preserve what he did.'

The church is Christ's body, *not* because it is visible and he is invisible (an idea often popularised by preachers but nowhere taught in Scripture) but because it is *linked to him* by shared life. It is also *subject to him* as limbs are subject to the head, each limb occupying its proper place and function in accordance with the head's wishes, and therefore each limb related healthily to every other limb. *That* is the implication drawn out of the actual Bible references to the body of Christ, as a glance at I Corinthians 12, Romans 12 and Ephesians 4 will show. The body metaphor teaches obedience to a present lord, not replacement of an absent lord. Continuing the metaphor, leaders are not the head, but fellow-limbs within the body.

Third, there are theological implications fraught with danger. It is not merely a matter of mixing metaphors. The spectres of medieval Rome and of modern heretical cults lurk here. The Reformers saw the papacy as an expression of Antichrist precisely because its religious hierarchy claimed control of the sacramental door to salvation. It interfered with the believer's assurance of salvation and denied his direct access to God. (The delightful fact that through 'renewal' many modern Catholics are finding that assurance and access again underlines that it was indeed lost, not that it was never really threatened.) In a slightly different way, the brainwashing pseudo-christs of some modern cults achieve exactly the same end. Their devotees depend for security, certainty, eternal life itself, on membership of the right organisation and submission to its leaders at every point. In both cases, religious leadership has *replaced Christ as the door*.

THE SHEPHERD AND THE SHEEP

John 10 contains a complex allegory. The essential parts are as follows, in order of appearance.

The sheepfold (verse 1) in which sheep are kept at night.
The thief and robber (verse 1) who 'does not enter by the gate, but climbs in.'
The shepherd (verse 2) who 'goes in through the gate.'
The gatekeeper (verse 3) whose task is to welcome the shepherd, 'open the gate for him,' and hand the sheep over to him in the morning.
The sheep (verse 4) who recognise the shepherd's voice when he calls them.
The gate (or door) (verse 7) which protects the sheep in the fold, and gives them entry and exit.
The hired man (verse 13) who is only in it for the money and has no time or concern for the sheep.

A slight experience of Middle Eastern shepherding (I have the advantage of living in Jerusalem where shepherds are seen every day) makes the meaning clear. The sheepfold is *the church*, and the sheep are *its members*. The shepherd is *Jesus*, characterised by the fact that he has ready access to the fold, is welcomed by any true *church leader* (the gatekeeper) and whose call is recognised and eagerly followed by the sheep. The gatekeeper's job is not to decide whether sheep can enter or not (what possible reason could there be for sheep *not* to enter the sheepfold?) but to open the way for the shepherd to call his sheep. The shepherd has immediate personal and direct access to the sheep, who each personally know his voice. There is always the danger of *false religious leaders* — the 'thieves and robbers' of verses 1, 8 and 10. They neither represent Christ the shepherd, nor are welcomed by the gatekeeper, nor are followed by the sheep (verse 5).

No metaphor, however rich, can fully convey the wealth of significance in the person and work of Jesus. So in verse 7 he claims to be not only the shepherd but also 'the gate for the sheep' (AV 'the door of the sheep'). Perhaps this reflects the fact that in the rough, roofless stone enclosures of Middle Eastern sheepfolds, the shepherd himself will sometimes sleep in the doorway at night. He is the first to sense danger; he is quite literally the door.

All this makes it quite clear what Jesus means by claiming to be both the shepherd and the door. He and only he can ever occupy these roles. They have nothing to do with his physical presence or absence in the world. Jesus 'calls his own by name and he leads them out' (verse 3) — as directly today as ever he did. They 'know his voice' (verse 4) in the same sense as they ever did — not recognising the timbre or modulation of his physical voice, but the irresistible spiritual power which says, 'Trust me; follow me; cast yourself upon me.' He is the 'good shepherd' because he was willing to 'die for his sheep' (verse 11). That truth is totally unaffected by his physical presence or absence, as the believing soul responds with joy and cries, 'He loved me and gave himself for me.' So he is the shepherd, and in no way can a church leader (or group of leaders) replace him.

But in the same way he is the 'door,' and in that respect too he needs and can have no replacement. Those who go in by him 'will be saved' (verse 9). I recall a man who listened to me preaching in an open-air meeting in Nottingham. He took a copy of John's Gospel which I offered to my hearers. He later wrote to me, 'I began to read the booklet through. When I got to Chapter 10 I read how Jesus said he was the door and anyone who entered in would be saved. There and then I prayed to him and entered in. I know he has saved me.' That man had a personal saving encounter with Jesus Christ. He never saw the physically absent Saviour. I acted as the visible agent, and my voice drew his attention to the Bible and thus to the Saviour. But in no way could I claim to have been 'the door'. At the very most I was the 'door-keeper!'

As *the door*, Jesus not only opens the way of salvation, but brings the sheep security, liberty and sustenance (verse 9 again). Precisely because he can be trusted to give access to the fold, the sheep can 'come in and go out and find pasture,' living a secure and liberated life. It is still the picture of a personal, direct and immediate relationship. The 'by me' of this great statement is emphatic in the original language. It is the main point of the sentence. By him, and by no one else, all this is effected. He, and no one else, is the door and no one else is the shepherd.

Why such strong language? Because Jesus' occasion for saying all this was the treatment meted out by *religious leaders* to one of his followers. A blind man's healing had brought him to faith in Christ (John 9). The Pharisees, enraged by the healed man's testimony, heckled him, argued with him, tried to persuade him to recant (verses 13–17), threatened his parents (verses 18–23), pronounced anathema on him (verse 28) and eventually '*expelled him from the synagogue*' (verse 34). They were claiming to be *the door* to worship and community for God's people. They tried to block the entrance to a true believer, and 'climbed over the wall' themselves. They showed themselves to be 'hired men' with much concern for their own establishment but none for the sheep. They used illegitimate means to hold power over God's people, employing threats and intimidation (expulsion from the synagogue would have quite crushing social and emotional implications as well as a religious effect). In fact Jesus was clearly referring to Ezekiel's devastating tirade against false shepherds (chapter 34) in the whole discussion. His hearers knew it. That is why they reacted so angrily. Ezekiel and Jesus both point from the false leaders to the true Shepherd. Their words are virtually identical in places, and any consideration of John 10 should include Ezekiel's tremendous picture, which makes the point that I am arguing here.

MISPLACED METAPHOR

Now I may seem to be labouring the point unduly. But the whole danger of the offending statement lies in the enormous emphasis and meaning attached to this concept of 'the door.' However unwittingly, if such a title with such implications is given to church leaders, a path is being pursued which is almost bound to lead to the very kind of situation reflected in house church horror stories.

The writer goes on to admit that some people have real problems in accepting authority and points out that they can always attend the public meetings of a restoration church without coming through the door into membership. On the other hand, they should not linger too long: 'there really isn't time to dally or to vacillate. God is extremely patient (read II Peter 3:9–12) but there is also an element of urgency in our day.'

Now this again has horrifying implications. The passage in Peter is indeed about the patience of God and the urgency of the day. But the issue is not membership of a church that has a particular pattern of leadership — it is about *whether we are saved or lost* — whether we are heading for Christ's recognition or his judgement at the second coming.

> The Lord is ... patient with you, because he does not want anyone to be destroyed, but wants all to turn away from their sins. But the Day of the Lord will come like a thief. On that Day the heavens will disappear.
>
> II Peter 3:9–10

Because 'the door' of Christ's salvation, opened by his hand, is confused with 'the door' of group membership controlled by the elders' hands, then salvation and escape from the wrath of God are being confused with the (understandable) safety and comfort of a select membership under a firm leadership.

This is exactly the impression given by a house church acquaintance who calmly related to me an opportunity to witness for Christ which he had found whilst waiting in a doctor's surgery. 'They were interested in the gospel,' he explained, 'but I did not pursue it because they were living in an area where there isn't a New Testament church.' No point in explaining the way of salvation if there isn't an authorised leadership to take over afterwards! In that case, Philip should not have led the Ethiopian eunuch to Christ! Structure and authority matter more than personal salvation. The door has changed its nature!

Now of course this chapter has quoted the views of only one house church writer. It would be unfair to tar the whole movement with one brush. Nevertheless the dangers here shown have kept recurring in every generation (and in very different types of movement). It is a warning to *all* of us.

The same thing happened to the medieval church. A reformer or a believer who had scriptural or conscientious reason to question the teaching and practice of the church found himself trapped in a situation where the door was being opened and closed by someone other than Christ. God's authority had been delegated to the Church, he was told. The sacraments supplied spiritual life, and the sacraments were controlled by the priest (who could, for example, 'command Christ to come down' upon the altar). The Bible was indeed the Word of God, but there was no point in his studying it (often he was forbidden to) because the religious hierarchy decided on its meaning and transmitted its authority. Obedience to God was encouraged, but was *defined* as obedience to God's delegated authority (priest, abbot, bishop, cardinal or pope, as the situation required). There was indeed comfort and security within this arrangement as long as the disciple could conform to it. But his access to God was closed, and his personal walk with God was put several removes away. Unless the Holy Spirit used the Word of God to disturb the conscience and stir the mind, he was in deep trouble. It was then that confessors and martyrs defied the authority, suffered its excommunication, endured its persecution, and took their comfort from their personal access to Christ and his personal communion with them. Their hymns and poems, their letters and books, their defiant message scratched on prison walls all proclaimed it. The official church had 'closed the door,' but their Saviour *was* the door, and they knew that they entered through him.

Note

1. Roy Trudinger, *Master Plan*, Olive Tree Publications, 1980, ch2.

CHAPTER TWELVE

How to Win Friends and Start a Cult

THE dangers of a leadership which usurps the place of Christ are painfully obvious and find frequent illustration, past and present. The people who institute such a move do not have to be villains; sincere enthusiasm for a course taken to excess can do the trick.

THE JUNGLE OF HERESY

The complex world of the cults illustrates the same danger in a slightly different way. Here is a veritable jungle. The older well-established groups like Jehovah's Witnesses and Mormons make quite heavy use of the Bible, and profess great faith in it. More recent movements like the Moonies use it at the introductory stage. Others again are really not religious at all, but avowedly owe their origin to a pseudo-psychological technique (examples are the older Christian Science and the newer Scientology). Yet others are forms of Hinduism and Buddhism, dressed up in a slightly westernised garb. Perhaps the most dangerous to our own church members are those which begin as genuinely Christian movements (as Jehovah's Witnesses once did, incidentally) and emerge from what one might call the far left of the house church movement or the evangelical churches. Such sects illustrate the dangers inherent in the hierarchical system, for *that is their most common and consistent feature*. 'The door' is exactly what every cult leadership claims to be. Faith in Christ for salvation (to which lip service or more is often paid in the early stages) is first of all amended and eventually replaced by submission to his delegated leadership (as it claims to be). Bible study (at first encouraged) becomes increasingly controlled by the local leader's direction of the group, the printed interpretations which accompany it, and the increasingly authoritative pronouncements and demands of the top leader. He eventually starts to claim infallibility, and his writings take on the character of holy scripture. Personal and private Bible study disappears, personal accountability to God is played down, obedience to the leadership becomes paramount. Sooner or later the pronouncements take on a wildness of error and near blasphemy. The occult and demonic take over. Adherents begin to leave, and find themselves threatened with a variety of pressures ranging from physical restraint to legal action, from emotional assault to threats of possession and insanity. This is a composite picture; the details vary from one movement to another, and the characteristics differ in intensity.

What has happened? Christ is no longer the door. Salvation is no longer the purpose of the door. Membership is defined as total acceptance of the leadership and its decrees.

WARNING SIGNS

I wish to be clear. I am not identifying this distressing scene with the house church movement in any of its branches. Its top leaders are godly men, lovers of the Bible, deeply concerned to apply New Testament principles and to rescue the church from half-heartedness, compromise and worldliness. But the dangers are implicit, inside and outside that movement, in some leadership theories. None of them is likely to deny that groups break off and go their own way, exaggerating principles like submission and plunging into error. None will deny that some individual second- and third-line leaders have slipped into arrogance, dictatorship, and the heady enjoyment of controlling other people's lives. Sympathetic observers wince when they see followers beginning to smack their lips over the enjoyment of belonging to the Little Despised Group, the Only Correct People, The True Church. Leaders in traditional churches committed to renewal and reform according to the word of God feel foreboding when they see private Bible study discouraged, the small discussion group declared to be the only way to know God's Word, theology and church history dismissed as irrelevant. Their foreboding increases when they hear of churches and areas named on maps as 'the only places where God is working.' The foreboding becomes fear when they see spontaneous prophecies or eldership instructions regarded as infallible, advice given to 'shut your Bibles and listen to this,' and top leadership pronouncements given a special authority as 'from the throne. The red light is shining, though not only in one kind of church.

THE PRACTICE OF 'COVERING'

'Covering' is a technical phrase now widely used and closely related to concepts of discipleship and submission. The theory is that every church member is related to and committed to every other member, and has a shared responsibility for mutual care and welfare. This is obviously true. More traditional churches badly need to get away from attitudes that limit 'fellowship' to sitting in rows inside the same building, and 'ministry' to something done by the paid clergy (or at most the church officers).

One can readily think of scriptures which make this point.

> Be humble towards one another, always considering others better than yourselves. And look out for one another's interests, not just for your own.
>
> Philippians 2:3–4

> Let us be concerned for one another, to help one another to show love and to do good. Let us not give up the habit of meeting together.
>
> Hebrews 10:24–25

No part of the body can say to another, 'I don't need you,' explains Paul:

> There is no division in the body, but all its different parts have the same concern for one another. If one part of the body suffers, all the other parts suffer with it; if one part is praised, all the other parts share its happiness.
>
> I Corinthians 12:25, 26

Some of the house groups in my last church carefully fostered this approach, so that within a small group there was a very deep level of shared support. They borrowed each other's cars and lawn mowers, held special prayer for any in particular need, rallied round with everything from baby-sitting to giving car-lifts to hospital, and generally offered the kind of everyday support which no busy pastor or elder could ever give if it was left to him. At a deeper level, too, they shared frankly in spiritual ups-and-downs, related experiences of temptation and conflict, searched the Bible together to get answers to life's questions. It was a clear expression of New Testament *koinonia*, and it greatly saddened me that some of our older traditional members saw no need for it and regarded the whole thing as very suspicious. In fact the method could be parallelled in every historical move of revival and spiritual expansion in the church, as we have seen.

LEADERS WHO ARE LED

The need for mutual covering and spiritual care is also acute at the leadership level. The pastoral ministry in a 'one man minis- try' can be desperately lonely. Sometimes the pastor will eagerly accept the man-at-the-top image imposed on him and begin to see himself as virtually infallible. Any querying of his policy or teaching he sees as an affront to God and an attack on God's ser- vant. More often the pastor will be well aware of his frailties, but has no one to turn to for support and advice. His congregation would be shocked at the discovery that a minister can have fears, temptations, low spells or difficulties with his wife. His elders, deacons, or wardens are seen as junior management rather than spiritual friends. His local or denomination clergy-fraternal is perhaps a place for talking shop or else a venue for the stilted pre- sentation of papers on theoretical subjects. His bishop or area superintendent, however willing to be a *pastor pastorum*, is in actual fact compelled to be an overworked administrator and bureaucrat who is only called in hurriedly when it is too late and the pastor resigns, or his wife leaves him, or he has a nervous breakdown, or his doctrinal speculations attract the notice of the local newspaper.

I have always had elders or deacons who were personal friends and in later years a pastoral team of full-time workers. Although in theory 'senior minister,' I have regarded myself as in covenant with my colleagues for mutual advice, support, rebuke, correc- tion, and the seeking of God's will. If this is what 'covering' means, I do not think that I would ever be willing to take on church leadership without it.

THE PERIL OF OVERSTATEMENT

However, in some circles a highly technical theory has evolved, which leads to some strange conclusions. A thoroughly good idea is enlarged into a rigid requirement. Absence of 'covering,' it is said, leads to spiritual disaster and interferes with the believer's relationship with God.

The idea was first popularised by Watchman Nee, one of the shining stars of China's short Christian story. Coming to the fore in the 1930s and 1940s, this dynamic and devout figure filled a truly apostolic role in pre-Communist China. Through his labours many churches were formed and loosely knit together as the Little Flock Movement. with a high view of church membership and a tendency to exclusivism and non co-operation with western missionaries, the Little Flock produced some of the churches and Christians most resistant to Communist infiltration and control after the Revolution. The whole of the latter part of Nee's life was spent in lonely courageous imprisonment, until his death in 1972. He became a symbol of Christian loyalty, defiance and martyrdom. Like the apostle Paul, he found the prison years became the great writing years, as much of his teaching was translated into English and had a wide influence in Europe and America.

Significantly, Watchman Nee's principles were in many points close to Darbyism, and the Exclusive Brethren cultivated his friendship during his visit to Britain.

Nee taught a very literal concept of the church as the Body of Christ. His English translations are not always easy to follow; the enigmatic phrases that westerners associate with the inscrutable orient come thick and fast. He speaks of members of the Body of Christ as not only being one, but 'becoming the oneness' and the 'oneness is God himself.' 'Body' becomes not simply a symbol or metaphor, but a literal reality, and the church is actually the presence of Christ on earth. (Most of us would rather say that the Holy Spirit is the presence of Christ on earth, and the church is the body through which he works.)

Such a high concept of course leads to strong authoritarianism. The scriptural injunction to 'hold fast to the head' is only fulfilled by being in subjection to the local church. Quite specifically, Nee says that a member must accept rebukes from the 'covering' fellow-Christians *even though his own conscience and reading of the Word of God seem to contradict them.*[1]

COVERED OR EXPOSED?

What happens if he does not? He is no longer 'covered' and is in a dangerous position of exposure to the devil's attacks, from which he would have been safe whilst under cover. Jerram Barrs states[2] that the position is this for Nee: 'If a believer stands alone simply as an individual before God seeking his will for his life, then he is subject to Satan.' To avoid the dire danger that comes from 'losing your covering,' you should submit every detail of marriage hopes, family planning, financial arrangements, moving house, etc., to the 'covering.'

To all those who believe this, and to the memory of Watchman Nee, I say:

Where in the Bible is such a teaching found? If it is more than simply the subjective experience of some, and is indeed a fundamental spiritual principle, why is it not clearly spelled out in Scripture, beyond possibility of misunderstanding? Does it not put the individual Christian in a position where he expects failure if he does not keep the rules? Where do the rules come from? What of that direct recourse to God which is the believer's inheritance of grace? What of that glorious biblical experience of the high priesthood of Christ, available to every saint?

> Before the throne my saviour stands;
> my friend, my advocate appears.
>
> My name is graven on his hands;
> and him the Father always hears.
>
> *This instant* now I may receive
> the powerful answer to my prayer.
>
> *This instant* now by him I live;
> his prevalence with God declare.
>
> C. Wesley

Was Wesley wrong? Was the writer to the Hebrews mistaken?

Here is the most acute danger. That direct line which the believer has, by grace, to the Father is denied or interrupted. His assurance of salvation begins to rest, not on Christ, but upon his position in the movement or his loyalty to some principle. His spiritual perception, that ability to be led by the Spirit which is the hallmark of the child of God (Romans 8:14), begins to atrophy through disuse. Whereas God sharpens the Christian's perceptions through Bible study, conscience, circumstances, spiritual gifts, chastisement, good advice, Christian fellowship and prayer, the cult demands only one thing: unthinking obedience to the leader's decree.

A MOVEMENT THAT LOST ITS WAY

The melancholy story of the Exclusive Brethren underlines all this. The original vision of the Brethren in the 1830s was a return to New Testament simplicity and an abandonment of sectarian labels. Their church structure found as its only necessary basis, Christ's promise to be present where two or three gathered in his name (Matthew 18 again). Shared ministry, 'open worship' and plural eldership characterised the early 'assemblies.' They maintained a high level of discipleship amongst their members, and a strong emphasis on 'separation' both from the godless world and from what they perceived as a compromising Christendom. Generally speaking, the Open branch of the movement has consistently maintained these principles. So God-honoured has been their work of Bible teaching, their world-wide evangelism, and (ironically) their provision of a stream of church leaders into most of the denominations, that other evangelicals can regard with equanimity the 'us and them' attitude which often slightly mars the assemblies' relations with other churches and Christians.

With the minority Exclusive break-away movement, the story has been very different. From the beginning there was a tension between the all-embracing 'gathered-to-his-name' approach of people like Anthony Norris Groves and George Müller (of Orphanage fame) and the exclusive 'come-out-from-among-them' principle of John Nelson Darby. A dynamic and colourful figure who abandoned ordination in the Anglican Church in Ireland, Darby built up a system of thought in which the 'Church Age' was seen as an experiment now abandoned by God, irretrievably ruined by the 'clergy principle.' The return of Christ was expected at any moment, and meanwhile believers must withdraw from the whole ruined system and establish groups bound together by a common commitment to Darby's view, led by lay readers responsible directly to God. The inevitable split between the two disparate tendencies came in 1848. Another leader, Benjamin Wills Newton, had given teaching in the Plymouth assembly which came into conflict with Darby in some fairly exotic detail of prophetical interpretation. Their personal animosity deepened when Newton went on to use obscure but unwise words to describe the humanity of Christ. Newton later withdrew the words, and in any case moved away from Brethren circles. However, Darby was angry with the Plymouth leaders for not actually expelling Newton, and when two of their perfectly innocent members moved house and joined the large assembly in Bristol, he attacked the Bristol leaders in turn for welcoming people guilty of heresy by association. Darby insisted on every assembly world-wide deciding for or against Bristol, and bewildered converts in Europe, the Middle East and India were required to give a verdict on an issue whose origins were obscure and whose continued existence was doubtful. The majority who declined to get involved remained as the Open Brethren, whilst the minority who accepted Darby's call for discipline became the Exclusive Brethren.

As the century passed, the principles of separation-from-all-error and guilt-by-association led to a succession of further divisions and sub-divisions amongst the Exclusives, each party developing a strong centralised government and giving to its respective leaders increasing authority as the only true exponents of Scripture.

The London party produced in the mid-twentieth century another dynamic leader, the American James Taylor (died 1970). Taylor greatly strengthened the power of local leadership to carry out his ever-increasing instructions about every area of personal and corporate life. Expulsion accompanied by social ostracism was meted out to those who questioned his authority or who jibbed at the increasingly odd demands. The instruction of II John 9–11 was taken to remarkable extremes and in some cases destroyed professional careers and broke up families. Newspaper notoriety was attracted when professional families were allegedly driven to suicide.

Meanwhile Taylor himself accepted the bestowal of more and more lavish titles upon him (I recall 'apostle' and 'archangel'). Virtual infallibility was attributed to his utterances. The movement reached its inevitable *dénouement* as charges of immorality and financial chicanery (unprovable, but indicating the depths of bitterness then reached) began to be made between leaders. By this time some features bore quite clearly marks of the demonic. That is hardly surprising; spiritual pride was, after all, the cause of Lucifer's fall.

The dismal tale encapsulates many of the warnings that need to be sounded about current trends. Notice the following features:

There is authoritarianism. The new leader, with charisma and zeal outclassing the traditionalists, attracts deserved devotion and an eager hearing and appoints second-line leaders in turn. For a while the freedom from all traditional restraint is intoxicating, but inevitably new disciplines become necessary, new rules and standards and jargon and techniques take over, and the very dedication inherent in a new movement requires stricter discipline than there was in the old.

There is exclusivism. Often at real cost, adherents have parted company with some older movement, or fresh converts are shown (with little difficulty) the faults of the old and the virtues of the new. Imperceptibly at first, then more overtly, the new movement becomes the 'only true faith' — the one ideal structure, outside whose ranks other Christians are dismissed as not being serious disciples (perhaps not Christians at all). Salvation is linked inseparably with membership of the True Church.

There is illuminism. The novel doctrines and fresh insights of the new leaders give them a reputation for originality and discernment. Increasingly exotic spiritualising of Bible passages is employed. The Reformers' principle of the obvious sense of Scripture is abandoned in favour of double meanings which would not have occurred to the unaided reader. Dependence on the leadership grows correspondingly, and the first rank begins to make claims for special revelation of various types. What the Spirit says through the leadership becomes more important than what the Bible says. Peculiarity becomes a positive virtue — does this not show that the clogging grave clothes of dead tradition have been abandoned?

There is priestcraft. By that I mean the interposing of human authority between the believer and his God. Direct communion with God is increasingly replaced by submission to the leaders, loyalty to the group, membership of the movement. The whole life is drawn from the corporate body rather than from God himself. Deprived of that body (by its disapproval, its excommunication, or its collapse) the devotee is bewildered and lost.

These, then, are some of the dangers inherent in excessive church discipline. The dangers find frequent illustration in history, and all of them are repeating themselves today. We have to steer between the Scylla of permissiveness and the Charybdis of authoritarianism.

Notes

1. Jerram Barrs, *Freedom and Discipleship*, IVP, 1983, p46, quoting from *The Body of Christ: A Reality*, New York, Christian Fellowship Publishers, 1978.
2. Jerram Barrs, op. cit., p47.

Part Four: The Problems
CHAPTER THIRTEEN

Cultures in Collision

TWO unmarried missionary women faithfully sowed the seed of God's word in a Central American jungle village. Several years passed and to their growing dismay they saw no conversions. They spent a day in prayer and fasting, seeking guidance from God as to what was the problem. Next morning at breakfast as they drank their usual lime juice, a native dropped in and asked a very pointed question. It led to a horrifying discovery. Lime juice was regarded by the local women as an after-sex contraceptive. The regular breakfast of the two ladies was widely regarded as evidence that they had spent the night with men. Their whole witness was undermined daily. They changed their breakfast diet, and began to see conversions.[1]

It would not occur to many that lime juice was a matter for church discipline, but in a particular culture it was decisive. The clash of cultures is one of the church's most pressing problems, as it seeks to maintain a witness and life style that is credible. Norms and accepted standards may differ widely. Endless misunderstanding may ensue. The church may find itself fighting the wrong battle in the wrong way — especially if the leadership is not indigenous.

A missionary doctor in Africa found that a patient had died through the neglect of a local Christian attendant who was drunk at the time. She suspended him. To her amazement she in turn was suspended by the local church and severely reprimanded for the sin of anger. This, to them, was by far the greater fault, especially as she was a *woman* who became angry with a *man*, a *white* woman who became angry with a *black* man. Here were toally contrasting values; the British middle-class horror of drunkenness and bad workmanship, coupled with a high value set on human life, in contrast with the African dislike of paternalism, distate for colour prejudice, sense of correct man-woman

119

relationship — and pietistic disapproval of anger thrown in.

CULTURE OR DEVOTION?

Of course we do not need to go to the mission field for illustration. The clash between values is at home too. A lady once asked
me if she would really be welcome in my church. Why not? I
asked. Because, in her search for God she had gone to another
chapel and been rebuked for wearing a trouser suit. I got rather
excited, and mentioned the incident in my next sermon. 'Let me
spell it out,' I said, getting rather rhetorical. 'God looks at the
heart, not the clothes. When we ask God to send in people to
hear the gospel, he is not sending them in to be like us. People are
welcome here wearing suits of armour or grass skirts if they wish.'
It caused a good deal of amusement, but some negative reaction
too. Little murmurs of disapproval were heard as young people
began to attend clad in jeans. Then came boys on motorbikes —
'and actually wearing leather jackets in church' — as one scandalised old lady exclaimed.

A few years later, when many such had become committed
Christians and regular worshippers, our church magazine editor
was interviewing me on my recollections. Obviously he was
reflecting various reaction to the stand I had taken. One question
went something like this: 'Don, you yourself have commented on
the general noise and lack of reverence at the beginning of our
services. You have recalled how you battled to establish a 'wear-
what-you-like' policy, and in your time we have seen the intro-
duction of 'renewal choruses' to supplement traditional hymns.
In retrospect, do you not think that these two factors have been
the main cause of the irreverence?'

The question was thoughtfully put, but it revealed serious confusion about reverence and its relationship to cultural factors. As
far as noise was concerned, some of the chief culprits were traditional elderly folk who arrived early and had a good gossip. They
always had, but now there were more of them, so more noise.
Yet in spite of the visual evidence, it was *assumed* that youth and
modern casual clothes makes for irreverence, and that age with
sober clothes makes for reverence. Likewise, it was *assumed* that
words of praise in modern metre and harmony are less worship-
promoting than Sankey or Watts hymns of a particular metre and
an older type of harmony. In actual fact, the things are not
directly related at all. A sober suit happens to be the cultural
expression of one age and class, carrying the message 'I respect
this church'. Informal dress is equally the cultural expression of

another age and class, bearing the message, 'I love this church and feel at home in it'. The same applies to the issue of musical style.

The culture may be neutral, or good or positively bad. African dancing is part of a genuine culture, so perhaps is appropriate to worship. But what if it has strong elements in it, either of the overtly sexual, or of the invitation to the occult? Then it would surely be out of place. In Britain, folk music and country-and-western music are natural vehicles for faith and feeling (though perhaps a little too pally, to my mind, for addressing God). On the other hand, heavy rock is so totally allied to an anti-God, anti-morality culture, with several of its leading exponents heavily into demonism, that to my mind it is unacceptable as a medium of worship or testimony. I have delayed baptism to young people who were not prepared to stop wearing jackets with the names and insignia of certain groups. It was not the leather that was at issue!

THE POLYGAMY PROBLEM

One of the most notorious and recalcitrant problems at the growing-edge of the world church is created by differing marriage customs. Polygamy is a totally accepted way of life to many. It does not always and necessarily go with the debasing of women or the exploitation of sex (though of course often it does). It is sometimes to do with security and care for women, especially of the elderly. When in one area polygamy was banned through church influence, men who had previously married (and thus cared for) the widows of older brothers or uncles, now smuggled them out of the area and sold them as slaves. Monogamy spelled the welcome cessation of a moral and social obligation.

Some missions in pioneer areas have insisted on a convert abandoning all but one of his wives. Affection and loyalty are not unknown, so great distress was caused when the edict was obeyed, or (more often) the converts held back and limped along without church fellowship because they found obedience impossible. One missionary put it in a neat epigram 'The good news about salvation was perceived as the bad news about polygamy.'

'No membership without dismissing all but the first wife' is sometimes the rule. What then happens to the others? A wealthy chief converted to Christianity built a small village for them and set up a community. Few can afford to do that. An alternative has sometimes been prostitution for the others. A by-product is a dichotomy between salvation and membership. Salvation is a matter of free grace in Christ; membership itself is work-oriented.

Now of course the New Testament is quite clear about polygamy. One-man-one-woman is the ideal, God's will declared in creation, and confirmed by Christ. Sex outside one's marriage is adultery. Adultery is one of the few scriptural reasons for outright excommunication. But is it as simple as that? Is a man brought up in polygamy with a perfectly clear conscience and subsequently brought to God, really in the same position as a Christian deliberately going into adultery? Does the grace of God stand helpless before a situation in which a man is trapped, without resource to a solution which may be as bad as the problem?

Many missions take a middle course, which commends itself to this author. They accept polygamous members on real evidence of faith and repentance, *and expect polygamy to disappear from that family in the next generation*. The sign of a better mind is not to jettison the victims, but to enlist their help in teaching their children the better way. Someone of the next generation who knowingly chooses polygamy would not be eligible for membership. Meanwhile, church *leadership* would be reserved for men untainted by the practice, though that, too, can be hard to endorse in an area of rapid growth. As a missionary asked me recently, 'What do you do when the most spiritually gifted and most obvious natural leader has three wives? Wait until two have died?'

SUCCESSIVE POLYGAMY

The permissive West has its similar problems in a different guise. Here it is divorce and remarriage which is institutionalised. The scale is now massive. In British evangelical churches divorce was almost unknown twenty years ago. Without any particular thought, it was assumed that a rare case of divorce within the church would lead automatically to resignation, and that an already divorced person would not apply would not, indeed be the slightest bit likely to develop any interest in spiritual things. In my first pastorate I never came across it, in the first half of my second pastorate it happened once, and in the second half a large crop of conversions brought a number. In my third pastorate, after a few experiences, I began to expect that people seeking God were likely to be already divorced — and I saw the first few examples of divorce amongst the already committed. In America, apparently, divorce amongst long-term church members is commonplace, and divorce in the ministry is described as epidemic. A leader whose missionary society draws candidates from both sides of the Atlantic has just told me that a major issue is the application of divorced candidates for the field — and the question of whether marriage breakdown for someone already in the field is sufficient cause for being sent home.

NO EASY ANSWERS

This writer believes that the Scriptures constitute the verbally inspired word of God, and contain all things necessary for our salvation, our spiritual growth, and the governing of our churches. That does *not* mean that a simple proof text is going to be all that there is to say on these issues. Two proof texts taken out of context and unnaturally linked together are even less likely to get us anywhere. It is not the way that Jesus dealt with the thirsty woman at Sychar's well, or with Zacchaeus, the Jericho tax collector. It is not the way that Paul dealt with the appalling problems in Corinth. This is a complex and explosive subject.

It seems to me that hard and painful thinking needs to be done. Church leaders at local level must be wiling to grasp the nettle. In a day of widespread breakdown of family, dare we do anything less than this?

Firstly, spell out the clear teaching of Scripture, making use of the research and conclusions of conservative thinkers who are committed to Biblical authority but are actually relating it to today's situation.

Secondly, encourage traditional believers to express and share their convictions but to apply to them *what the Bible actually says* — not just to what their grandparents said, or what their childhood chapel said. At the same time, encourage new Christians trapped in insoluble situations before conversion, to share their experience. Of course this is dynamite. To a vicar or pastor accustomed to his P.C.C. or Church Meeting going up in flames over the colour of the Sunday school carpet or the choice of the choir's anthems, coming to grips with issues like this sounds like an invitation to civil war and bloodshed. In that case, let us face it — we are dismally failing to be the reconciled community, the People of God, and are simply a holy huddle of like-minded ostriches. It is time to fast and pray.

Thirdly, just that. call a day of prayer, and seek God.

Fourthly, work out some tentative policies in the rabbinical manner, relying on the promise of Christ's presence with his people — and with the basic assumption that new beginnings are found at the cross, and that every member is at best a sinner becoming a saint because God has declared him (in Christ) to be saved and sanctified. Don't reduce it to a rule book. If there must be formality, make it a series of resolutions to look at again in the light of further experience. In other words, believe and practise Matthew 18.

GETTING OUR LINES CROSSED

Another story illustrates two different points. Missionary leaders of a church in India were alarmed by the increase of unmarried pregnancies in the church. What was most disturbing, the local elders avoided every appeal to tackle the issue until one day a missionary in a letting-your-hair-down mood began to talk about petting problems in the youth fellowship of his American home church. The startled elders exclaimed, 'Then *you* have moral problems too!' and then poured out their own concern for the local situation. In the course of the frank discussion they told the missionaries that one of the causes of the illegitimate births was the mission's own Western-oriented education policy, which forbade marriage before graduation. Delayed marriage led to intense temptation, which in turn led to immorality.[2]

Here was a communication blockage (in both directions) because of different values. The elders thought that the missionaries claimed a problem-free experience — and at the same time distrusted them. The continuing East African Revival in fact constantly reveals and resolves a hitherto unsuspected problem. Reciprocal openness, we could call it. Public confession of faults and restitution play a large part. The natives thus surmount what was previously an immense problem; they had imagined that missionaries were supposed to have no faults, yet saw with painful clarity that it was not so. Now it is openly acknowledged and co-operation is possible.

A friend of mine went to pastor a large Baptist church in the West Indies. His horrified discovery of the immense number of illegitimate births in church circles almost destroyed his sanity. There was in fact a mutual misunderstanding. The populace saw formal marriage, with a ceremony and a document, as a middle-class feature. If and when they reached a certain financial standing, partners already committed to each other and living together marked their graduation to the moneyed class by getting married — usually in their forties, accompanied by their grown children. Incidentally, I confirmed whilst preaching in Europe that there are still rural areas where good evangelical Protestants like to make a witness by having a marriage ceremony when their first child is expected. To them the ceremony is the liturgical confirmation, but the reality is their decision to live together in loyalty and love — marked by getting on with it. I believe that the Service for the Solemnisation of Holy Matrimony in the old English Prayer Book was originally seen in very much the same light — the cultic declaration of what was already a fact.

Walter Trobisch has gone so far as to suggest that the most fundamental tragedy of the African church is that Western leaders and African members are totally at cross-purposes when it comes to an understanding of marriage and of sexuality. They are simply not hearing each other. Each notices the sound of the words that the other is using, but cannot attach meaning to them. He suggests that to an African, words like 'faithfulness' and 'adultery' have no real meaning. 'Sexuality' and 'love' can mean the same thing to an African, but to a western missionary 'sexuality' and 'sin' mean the same thing — so the missionary is perceived as saying that *love is sin*.

Moreover, (he says), the African mind is not concerned with *guilt* but with *shame*; the shame being to be found out in the sin and humiliated. The real error is to be discovered and punished. But his psychology is also leader-oriented. He is deeply attached to authority — whether in village chief or pastor. He thinks of 'palavers' (prolonged verbal trials) with a good deal of pleasure. The Westerner has taught him that he (the African) is an irrational, immature child. His own pastor cheerfully accepts the diagnosis — for his people if not for himself. Church discipline thus becomes a set-piece trial, a kind of exercise in ecclesiastical litigation, with evidence, verdict and punishment all in due course. Trobisch quotes the Lutheran Chruch in Madagascar (1960) for examples of this discipline in action. It is an extraordinary mixture of village tribal palaver and Western democratic legal processes. The church is a bailiff acting for God, the church council a morality squad, and the pastor a kind of heavenly prosecuting counsel. Punishments include exclusion from communion, fines in money or goods, manual labour, private or public confession, re-attendance at catechismal classes, penal seats, public reproof and excommunication.

It is a startling picture. I am in no position to vouch for its accuracy. Trobisch himself argues against the whole system on four grounds. First, only God can reform; the effort of men to do so will lead to a legal system, not an experience of grace. Second, the Saviour's parables like the Weeds and the Net (Matthew 13)

125

teach that he, not we, will do the separating. Third, the word and the sacraments alone are sufficient to produce any meaningful discipline, for they convey God's grace. Fourth, the only valid witness which the church can hope to make is 'a pure proclamation, not a pure reception'.

This is interesting, because he is (consciously or not) faithfully repeating the arguments of the early Protestant Reformers against the Radical Reformation — that is, against the Matthew 18 pattern and the voluntary principle. A collection of cultural factors has trapped him in the very position to which the Reformers were driven by quite a different culture.

The fourth point is as idealistic and unbiblical as it was when the Reformers first made it. Past history and present experience simply do not indicate that sound preaching and proper sacraments are sufficient. Nor does the New Testament. Go to your brother. If necessary take witnesses. If still necessary share it with the whole church. If even then still necessary, withdraw from the offender. Matthew 18 says all that. The apostle Paul took the Corinthian Christians (leaders and led) to task for simply leaving things to find their level in a church with apostolic preaching and striking gifts. 'Deal with the situation, or I shall, and worst of all, God will,' is a fair summary of his message (see I Corinthians 5).

In actual fact, Trobisch's words quoted are unfair to himself. He is renowned for his meticulous, compassionate counselling to thousands of people (face to face or by correspondence). The point he is making is that people are *human beings* for whom Christ died, not cases for discipline. A book of rules may be very like the Talmud, but is assuredly *not* what Jesus is promoting when he makes his Matthew 18 promises. At the slow patient level of face-to-face sharing, frank exchange and reverent seeking of God's will, Christ's presence 'in the midst' will be experienced, prayer will be answered, wise moment-by-moment decisons made, and reconciling love displayed. As Trobisch says, the Bible does not legislate about polygamy; it brings a message to polygamists. One might add, for a different culture, that the New Testament does not legislate for divorce; it brings a message to divorcees. Some of our traditional members might prefer to believe that a few words in the Sermon on the Mount *are* divorce legislation and leave no more words to be said. Yet they themsleves would be very hard put to it if the immediately surrounding words were likewise turned into legislation. Hell fire for calling a man a fool? Excommunication for losing your temper? Suspended from communion for failing to give your coat to a beggar? Name read out on Sunday for pointing out motes in your brother's eye? Oh dear no — these are general principles and illustrations, not legalistic rules, we all hurriedly say. Quite so. All of them. Even the one about divorce. Or shall we make them rules after all, and the elders set up a court to examine the brethren on the impure thoughts that they may have had about the girls since last Sunday?

A WAY FORWARD

How can the local church and its leadership apply firm but loving discipline which escapes the snare of traditional-culture legalism but avoids the pitfall of permissive-culture libertarianism?

1. We must return to Bible absolutes. They are there, and they are not too numerous. They must be taught, not as rules, but as expressions of the will of a holy and righteous God.

2. We must carry people with us. God's purpose is not instant-saints, except in the sense that at conversion he *declares* us to be saints. There then begins a process of becoming-what-you-are; the key to New Testament ethics. Sanctification, not legislation, is the principle. Inward renewal, not outward conformity, is the aim.

3. We must call on all the resources of training, teaching, counselling, example, exhortation, fellowship and leadership that are available.

4. We must be patient. This generation carries the entail of the past. Give God time to work in two or three generations.

5. We must act within a framework of *grace*. This is the whole basis of New Testament Gospel, and church membership cannot be narrower than the Gospel. We receive people because Christ has received them (Romans 15:7). Christ received them (and us) as sinners, not waiting for them to be what they should be, but going to them where they were, immersed in what they should not be. New converts must be offered the new start in membership of the church which the gospel offers in membership of the Family of God. If what they have done wrong can be put right then let this be done. Zaccheus did that (Luke 19:1–10). If it cannot, then their sincere repentance must be taken as the sign of grace received, even if they cannot put it right. Jesus treated the woman at the Samaritan well that way, with her five divorces and her sixth man (John 4:16–18). Did she marry the sixth one after her conversion, or leave him? Certainly, either way, she could not cease to be a divorced woman. Yet within an hour she was a highly successful personal evangelist (verse 39). Is it seriously

conceivable that she never became a church member?

6. We must always regard church discipline of a member who stumbles and offends after conversion as *a route to restoration*. 'It is enough that this person has been punished.... Now ... forgive him and encourage him, in order to keep him from (giving) up completely' (II Corinthians 2:6–7).

7. We must distinguish between the standards immediately expected of leadership, and eventually expected of membership. Paul clearly does so by listing the qualifications for eldership and diaconate when writing to younger leaders (e.g. I Timothy 3:1–13). This is unavoidable. The famous saying 'Do as I say, not as I do,' cannot be on the lips of Christian leaders. Rather, we must say with Paul 'Imitate me, then, just as I imitate Christ' (I Corinthians 11:1).

Notes

1.   Harold Fuller, *Mission-Church Dynamics*, William Carey Library, 1980.
2.   'The Christian Encounter with Culture' in *World Vision Magazine* (1967).

CHAPTER FOURTEEN

People and Structures

IT used to be said that a bad workman always blames his tools. Like many sayings, it is only partly true. Equally, a good workman needs good tools. In the matter of church discipline, we need to take a realistic look both at the workmen and the tools, in other words at the people who staff our churches, and the structures we inherit. Leadership patterns, styles of government, deacons' meetings, parochial church councils, presbyteries, synods: these are our tools. Church leaders and members: these are our workmen. There is a vital link between structure, education and discipline.

LEADERSHIP PRESSURES AND PERILS

The Holy Spirit is the dynamic personal power in the church — but he chooses to use human beings. I used to think it rather spiritual to deny this, but the Spirit himself affirms it. Why else would he call Moses, Joshua, Samuel and David? Where otherwise was the need for Isaiah, Nehemiah and Ezra? Why did Peter, John, Paul and Timothy not leave it all to the Holy Spirit? Why does every period of revival, reformation and renewal throw up its human pioneers and key figures? Why Martin Luther, John Wesley, Martyn Lloyd-Jones and David Watson?

A great reponsibility rests on church leaders, at every level. For better or worse, churches take on the standards and expectations of their leaders — whether or not they are ordained clergy!

There have always been three types of leadership. There is the *institutional*, which finds its clearest expression in Catholic circles. Whatever they are called (bishops, apostles, superintendents), institutional leaders exercise their authority through their position in the hierarchy. They are listened to because they have inherited or appointed power. The reaction to institutional leadership is, 'This is right and that is wrong because my church tells me so.' In a day of open-ended debate, subjectivism and permissiveness, there is an obvious need for it in some form. It is the kind that is expressed in inter-church relationships, where discipline often falls down. Mr Brown switches from playing squash to playing golf; Mr Smith switches his support from Spurs to Arsenal; Mr Jones switches his membership from Independent Methodist to Free Baptist. It is a buyer's market, and the competing churches are eager to sell him their membership. Churches, whether of the same denomination or different, should discourage transfers that are mere escapes from discipline. In a small town I found this worked well between Parish Church, Free Church and Brethren; we consulted each other about such cases instead of working against each other. A wandering member did not dodge responsibilities simply by changing his membership.

Secondly, there is the *educational*. This is the normal Protestant expression of leadership. The leader's main task is seen as teaching, preaching, imparting knowledge of the word of God. The pastor (teacher, minister, elder) leads with Bible in hand. The reaction to educational teaching is, 'I know *this* is right and *that* is wrong because the Bible says so.' In a day when any opinion goes, this is badly needed. Its discipline is expressed in teaching, training, and preservation of sound doctrine.

Thirdly, there is the *inspirational*. This finds its most obvious expression in Pentecostalism. Charisma, ability, gift, personality, persuasiveness, inspiration and example: these are the traits of the inspirational leader. The reaction is, 'I know *this* is right because I feel it, I see it demonstrated, I am moved and persuaded by it.' The leader gains his following because he is loved, emulated, admired.

In fact the church needs all three kinds of leadership. There will be obvious tensions between them, but they can be perfectly creative tensions. Or the opposite.

The ministry must have respect restored to it. The leadership must know how to handle the Bible. The leader must enthuse and inspire, by deed and example. Ministers must abandon mere professionalism yet recover the sense of awe at their calling. They must break out from the fear of training and releasing second-line leaders who can do some things better than they can. They must create enthusiasm and expectation.

ELDERS — THE CASE FOR AND AGAINST

The revival of *eldership* is one of the most significant factors in today's British churches. It has come to so many, and for such varied reasons.

Calvinists want elders. Geneva had them; true enough. But the reason is more fundamental. The reformed faith sees the urgent need for pure Bible teaching applied to local church life. The New Testament seems to put that task in the hands of the elders.

Charismatics want elders. Their search is for a quickened laity, widely distributed gifts, the multiplying of small informal groups. This requires many unordained leaders of the inspirational type. In other words, elders.

Church-growth buffs want elders. Principles of group-dynamics make it necessary. A one-man ministry is more likely to create a bottleneck than a channel of blessing. That means either a remarkably large pastoral team (in most British churches financially impossible) or an eldership!

Household churches want elders. Fastest growing wing of Britain's church life, they have thrown up new patterns and theories of pastoral care and church discipline. The key is large numbers of lay leaders, each responsible for a small number of members. Whatever the verb employed (shepherding, caring, covering) they are in fact talking about a form of eldership.

Anglicans want elders. The age-old concept of 'vicar at the centre of the parish' represents a ministry to a village community. In the sprawling densely populated urban areas it almost completely fails to work. Although there seems to be no theoretical place for lay eldership in the Anglican system (unless it is the P.C.C.), increasing numbers of clergy are cheerfully mobilising what are in fact (and sometimes in name) lay elders on pastoral teams or in their house groups. I believe that many Catholics are experimenting with the same concept, for the same reason.

Traditional Free Churches want elders. It is a major talking point. They are recovering their earlier vision of shared ministry, and breaking out of the Victorian mould of pulpit giants and one-man ministry. 'Deacons' seem not to meet the new needs. Deacons have largely become known as administrators, welfare workers and guardians of the fabric and the constitution — all very laudable and necessary, but lacking something when it comes to teaching, caring, small-group leadership and the feeding of the local flock. Nonconformists have suddenly noticed that the New Testament speaks of elders *and* deacons, that they are not the same thing, and that a lot more is said about the first than the second.

Elders' duties are fairly clear in the many New Testament references. (I assume that *presbyteroi* and *episcopoi* are virtually the same thing in the New Testament, as Acts 20 suggests. The same group of men are described in both terms — 'elders' in verse 17 and 'guardians' (RSV) in verse 28.) Their task is variously described as shepherding, teaching, steering, ruling, protecting from false doctrine. They were appointed in infant churches almost immediately after the churches were established. They were expected to be men of exemplary character, able to teach, worthy of honour, and able to guide their own families as evidence that they could guide the church family (Acts 14:21–23; I Timothy 3:1–7; Hebrews 13:17). Their qualifications were rather more than those of deacons, and the differences suggest that their task was more specifically spiritual. (It is often asserted that the seven men appointed in Acts 6 by common consent were 'deacons' because they 'served at tables' but the Bible does not actually say so — and the only two of whom we have any further details were in fact powerful evangelists). Although 'elders' and 'bishops' seem to be the same, 'deacons' (translated 'helpers' in the Good News Bible) are clearly different (Philippians 1:1 and I Timothy 3:1, 8).

Why distinguish between elders and deacons? Many churches seem to find that difficult. A simple answer would be to say merely 'because the Bible does.' One might add, 'because pragmatic considerations require it.' In a church growing as it should, with elders and deacons meeting frequently and then scattering to perform their duties, a deacon occupied with fabric and finance (for example) can ill afford to spend hours consulting with an elder occupied (for instance) with pastoral care and church discipline, and vice versa.

Objections to elders. There is a lot of unease about newly emerging elders in local churches. Some of it is understandable. Elders *can* threaten the authority of the church meeting. They *may* relegate faithful deacons to being mere messenger boys. They *might* rally round a pastor and create a determined power base from which a bewildered church is steered along paths (theological or practical) which it neither wants nor understands. They *have been known* to turn into local dictators. They *could possibly* create a new élite within the church (an oligarchic meritocracy as one Baptist minister earnestly warned me). All of this is true. It not only could happen, but it has happened. There are worse dangers too, when some elders or shepherds gain a totally unjustified control over the souls of believers, and even interfere with the individual's personal access to God. But none of this, surely, is of the essence of eldership. How can it be, when the New Testament condemns all of these excesses, but contends for eldership?

In actual fact (let the melancholy truth be told) all of these excesses can be found in an ecclesiastical system, under any name. Deacons are certainly not immune to any of them. And who has not come across the figure of the church secretary or churchwarden whose attitude is, 'Ministers come and go, but I am the one who remains unchanging, and I have the real power'? In my own experience, two tendencies are evident amongst elders. Yes, they can become too powerful and a little too sure that they know what is best for the church. They can also slip into being mere administrators and rulers, rather than pastors and shepherds. That is because they are human, not because the office of elder carries with it a sinister influence. The answer to bad elders is good elders — biblical elders.

LONELY LEADERSHIP

A British church leader has said, 'It is my personal opinion that many ministers leave churches ... because they simply cannot face the burden of dealing with difficult situations on their own. They lack the support and security that is scriptural.'[1] I believe he is right. A pastor carrying on a lone crusade for Biblical standards and discipleship can have his heart broken or his will destroyed by seeming to be the man from outside rashly trying to change everything, or getting unwittingly entangled in local complications he doesn't understand. ('He doesn't *realise* that the little individual glasses were presented in memory of Mrs Featherhead, so we can't use a common cup the way he thinks the Bible says.' 'Yes, maybe young Brian Blenkinsop does have doubtful morals, but his uncle was a life-deacon.' 'Silly man, preaching on election and predestination when our best financial giver comes from a Salvation Army background.') And incidentally, in that lonely position the pastor will often go too far, demand too much, and behave rashly.

There is something about a body of church officers committed first of all to maintenance, finance and organisation(whether it is called a diaconate, a parochial church council or a church board). It instinctively and quite understandably represents the status quo, and carries a 'do-not-disturb' sign. What is needed to supplement that, and work alongside it, is a body of genuinely local people who understand and reflect the church but are committed to the vision of a holy people, to growth in discipleship, to discipline. Such a body supports the pastor, works with him, and keeps him realistic.

WHAT'S IN A NAME?

The eldership best expresses that in New Testament terms. But of course if the word 'elder' raises suspicions or stirs up unpleasant memories, then the principle is more important than the name. If Elders & Deacons do not sound right for local or denominational reasons, try Leaders & Helpers, or Pastors & Managers, or Pastoral-Deacons & Admin-Deacons, or Shepherds & Stewards. All of these twosomes fairly accurately reflect the quite clear roles assigned in the New Testament.

PARTNERS NOT RIVALS

What some churches understandably fear is a new élite of the superspiritual, rivalling the time-honoured and faithful servants of the past (deacons, stewards, sidesmen, wardens or whatever). Both the Reformed and the charismatic wings have in fact fallen into that folly fairly often. I have watched it happen to a young colleague in his first pastorate more than once. He comes into a happy but not very lively church, with a burning zeal for fifteen-point sermons à la Thomas Watson — or a determination to graft the Five Points of Calvinism onto a bewildered church in the first six months — or a scheme for throwing out the hymnbook and introducing overhead projector, choruses and singing-in-the-Spirit at his third church meeting — or public healing services every fortnight — or whatever. He gathers four or five equally young men around him and imposes on a bewildered membership a new order of leaders far younger than the trads (who are left to look after finance and leaking ceilings), all with an implacable resolve to change everything and a slightly frightening certainty that they have the Bible exclusively on their side. There are several aternative scenarios from then onward. The keen-new succeeds at the expense of the hurt-old, who drift away to another church or stop going anywhere (pursued by the cheery assertion that you always have to empty a church before you fill it — pastorally, one of the most irresponsible things I've ever heard said, but often hear). Alternatively, the forces of status quo rally and rebel, and there is a fight in which either the church is divided or (if they are Nonconformists) the pastor resigns and becomes a brush salesman or a social worker.

Both kinds of leadership should be in partnership, not rivalry. Perhaps they can be united in one court of elders and deacons, or something similar. In my observation that usually means that spiritual matters have to be placed well down the agenda. There is always something which, on the surface, *must* be looked at first. The boiler has broken down in mid-winter, or the Sunday school pianist has broken her leg, or last month's collections were down fifteen per cent. By half past nine, the committee is looking at less easily definable things like the spiritual state of the youth work, or fears that two church members are having an affair, or queries about the effectiveness of membership preparation. Ah well, it is getting late and we are all tired; let's put it top of the agenda next month. But next month several windows have been broken by vandals, and the Women's Fellowship is asking advice about a new constitution, and so on.

Better, I suggest, to have the two bodies regarded *together* as a basic building-brick in the structure, meeting perhaps quarterly for both fellowship and consultation, and to preserve a common sense of vision and direction, *agreeing* on allocated duties to be carried out separately.

A SUGGESTED MODEL

I sketch this out with a special emphasis on the Baptist, Brethren, Pentecostal and Independent type of church structure, with their emphasis already present on lay leadership and church-meeting-type participation. Without too much difficulty I imagine it could be adapted by presbyterian or parish structures.

i) *Membership Meeting* held monthly or quarterly in an atmosphere of prayer, worship and Bible study. Leaders at all levels are elected here, and present their reports here. Schemes for activity and advance in the church may come either as proposals from leaders or as requests for advice from leaders, or as suggestions from the general membership. The emphasis should not be on lobbying or voting, but on seeing God's will expressed in a sense of harmony and common direction.

135

ii) *Joint Leadership Meeting* held quarterly, shortly after a membership meeting when appropriate — or to prepare for a membership meeting soon to be held. Prayer, fellowship, sharing of vision, reports of progress. The leaders agree between themselves their respective areas of responsibility.

iii) *Separate Leaders' Meetings* separated by a rough distinction between administration and pastoral care.

'Deacons' (by whatever name) deal with finance, fabric, use of the premises, organisations, correspondence, needs of the departments, youth clubs, social welfare, relief work, organised visitation, etc.

'Elders' (by whatever name) deal with evangelism, public worship, visiting preachers, staffing of the departments, progress of house groups, membership preparation, spiritual state of the church, doctrinal questions, specific pastoral needs, progress of catechists or enquirers, accusations or fears about erring members. The final three in my list should in fact have a high priority at every meeting.

Should these tasks be compartmentalised? With deacons, obviously yes; one to act as treasurer, one as secretary, one to keep an eye on property and repairs, one to channel money and action into specific social needs, and so on. With elders I am not sure. There is great advantage, for example, in one elder moving amongst the house groups, one running a visitation scheme, one providing resources for public worship, etc. On the other hand, if every elder has a specific task like this he will be overworked and have little time for general pastoral care. Perhaps several should have allocated tasks, and several others be left free for visitation and general pastoral care. Perhaps those with an allocation could each be responsible for three or four families too, whilst those without would have more families, perhaps a dozen each. Incidentally, in a church of any size this is going to mean a large number of elders, and that in turn lessens the oft-expressed fear of the eldership becoming a small tight group of pastor's yes-men or a tiny élite committed to some special trend or policy.

The leaders (of both types) should be *elected* by some scheme which tests the membership's confidence in them. They should be required to stand down and offer themselves for re-election at intervals of a few years. They should verbally express their willingness to accept non-re-election (if it happens) *not* as a personal slight but as an indication of the flexibility and growth of the church. They should not be locked into a rule which limits their number artificially. Their number, rather, should be determined by present needs, present gifts, and present availability, in full consultation with the membership. It is utterly absurd for a church to have a need for a certain number of elders, for God to have clearly provided them, but for their election to be rendered impossible (as I have sometimes seen) because the number is greater than that specified in some previously made rule. Look for the church's need, God's provision, and a general recognition that certain people are already doing the work of elders and displaying the qualities of elders in an informal way.

SHARING RESPONSIBILITY WITH THE WHOLE CHURCH

There are enough New Testament references to 'every member leadership' to make the reader at least aware of it. Jesus' instruction to 'tell the whole thing to the church' (Matthew 18:17) we have already examined. 'The apostles and elders, together with the whole church,' took decisive action in the debate about circumcision and the gospel (Acts 15:22). The careless Corinthians were urged by Paul to deal with scandalous immorality 'as you meet together' (I Corinthians 5:4). Different churches give expression to this in various ways. The Parochial Church Council amongst the Anglicans, the Circuit Meetings amongst Methodists, the Church Meeting of Baptists and Congregationalists: with varied theological emphasis, these gatherings express some degree of shared responsibility and whole-membership participation.

There is, unfortunately, a wide gap between the ideal picture and the real thing as it works in practice.

Independents invented the technical phrase, 'church meeting.' For their shocking habit of meeting together in prayer and debate to find God's will, they were hounded out of England and built the American democracy. Congregationalists inherited it, and in more tolerant days built a denomination, founded a world mission, and produced the phrase 'the congregational form of church government.' Baptists eagerly embraced it, and gave it a mystique all their own. Next only to baptism with much-water-and-believers-only, the church meeting is their most prized possession. Christians of all shapes and sizes in the twentieth century have taken it happily into their systems, though not with quite the same burning conviction. For the purpose of this discussion, the phrase *church meeting* is simply a general term, with no sectarian connotations.

Trainee ministers are often assured that its preservation and practice are crucial to their ministries and the survival of their churches. Nowadays they are apparently given a little lesson in how to conduct its mysteries. A young friend of mine missed that lesson through a bout of influenza. In the first eighteen months of his initial pastorate he went through agonies of private embarrassment and public humiliation, because he could never grasp how to present a proposal, how to second a recommendation, and why you have to vote on an amendment before you vote on the original proposal, but then still have to vote on the proposal afterwards.

Which brings me to my point. However did we get from *there* to *here*? By what process did the glowing promise of Christ's presence in the midst of his people turn into an imitation of a trade-union committee meeting dominated by the religious equivalent of Bennite activists?

The Master's mandate for his church in Matthew 18 is shown again and again to be a key to church government and discipline, but how has *that* become an exercise in pseudo-democracy which most pastors dread — an obstacle which must regularly be surmounted or circumvented so that God's will can be done? The present General Secretary of the Baptist Union, whilst pleading for its renewal, talks of the need to be liberated from its 'democratic tyranny.' A very perceptive paper, issued by Mainstream — Baptists for Life and Growth, uses some stinging phrases, whilst also pleading for its renewal.

> Far from being the high point of church life, it is in fact the low point — the time when 'members' who participate in precious little of a spiritual nature in the church turn out to exercise their constitutional rights, and usually against what God is doing.

> Many of us find it hard to reconcile the obsession with procedure and correctness and propositions and voting that prevails in many churches with anything we read in the New Testament.[2]

Learning the hard way. My first church (F.I.E.C.) managed with a quarterly meeting. My second (B.U.) had it monthly. My third (B.U. but Interdenominational, the board said) needed it monthly but I could never get it more than quarterly. The majority of members and officers felt that was enough, thank you — the strain monthly would have been too much to cope with. Very few of our meetings were unhappy, and there were moments of high vision and spiritual power. Yet we all knew that the gap between this and Matthew 18 was so wide that we felt self-conscious about linking the two principles.

For most of my clerical colleagues, it seemed to be much worse. In connection with my own church meetings, I usually spent the morning before with the church secretary, the afternoon before on my knees in prayer over the agenda, and the following night wondering if I should take a sleeping tablet. For many of my colleagues (judging by anecdotes at clergy fraternals) it was a nightmare. Members never seen at a prayer meeting gathered to outwit the minister or outvote the deacons. People adept at bureaucratic procedure (income tax officers, local councillors and the like) made a sport of tying up the meetings in red tape. The rule book or constitution was deftly wielded whilst the Bible stayed shut.

HOW WE GOT HERE

Matthew 18 gives a picture of the realised presence of Christ amongst his obedient people as they harmonise in prayer, in an atmosphere of deep mutual commitment. Since every Christian is indwelt by the Holy Spirit, the best way to find God's will for Area A is for the Christians in Area A to get together and seek it — not to pass the matter on to presbytery B, Central Committee C, or even Bishop D. Simplicity, expectancy, freedom and mutual dependence are the keynotes.

Our forefathers fought that one out, against worldly clerics and all-powerful kings who saw the church as an arm of the state. That is why they became the first democrats, though not by deliberate design.

When they had won the right, at high cost, they had to find ways to exercise it. Naturally, in doing so they reflected their own cultures — those of the Victorian middle class, the American frontier, the emerging Labour Party. In England we produced a collection of pragmatic rule-of-thumb procedures — the 'normal procedures for conducting business' as some church constitutions actually call them. To some traditional people these 'rules' (as they became) appear to be the only way to conduct a Christian gathering for decision making. The *institution* (quite unknown to those far off forefathers and still less known to the disciples of Jesus in Galilee) has taken the place of the *principle*.

139

BASIC PRINCIPLES — AND HOW THEY WORK

What does the biblical 'church meeting' actually stand for? And how does it work in a modern church anxious to preserve (or discover) its value without being trapped in its traditional 'procedures'?

1. Freedom. Only a conviction freely arrived at can be called faith. That is why the Nonconformist rides rather loosely to the historic creeds and confessions. It is not a matter of disliking dogma, or of not belonging to the universal church. Many free churchmen take the actual spirit and content of, say, the Apostles' Creed as seriously as those who chant it every week! But they have a kind of race memory of creeds enforced and imposed as tests of orthodoxy. Not so very long ago you could not vote for parliament, or send your son to grammar school, or meet to pray, unless you accepted the form of words. And if you *did* accept the form of words, it sometimes looked very much as if you needed to do nothing else. So God's people gather together in freedom, in covenant relationship with one another, obedient to God's Word, interpreting God's will as the presence of Jesus is made known in Holy Spirit guidance.

2. Responsibility. How awesome to claim to speak in the name of Christ! It throws each Christian back on the only hope of getting it right; a humble, holy walk before God. That means submission to his book, fellowship with his people, and partnership with trusted and proven spiritual leadership. Responsibility springs from accountability. When people choose their pastors and other officers, raise the necessary finance for their support, and carry the can if things go wrong, then they are going to act responsibly.

3. Authority. Every democrat soon finds that order is necessary. A system in which everyone has his own way is an absurdity and indeed an impossibility. Rules, leaders, working compromises, give-and-take; all this is necessary. A free church hammers out its own rules, agrees them, appoints its leaders, and gives them all the more authority because the leaders are responsible horizontally to the people and vertically to God. In reality, of course, an Anglican church does too even if its structure at first sight hides that fact. The leaders assess both the needs and the hopes of the people. They know that a volunteer is worth ten pressed men. They know that energy will be used up positively in united action, or negatively in quarrelling and disagreement.

'The Holy Spirit and we have agreed', they said naïvely, when meeting to settle an early issue (Acts 15:28). That quotation is a useful one, for it comes at the end of a debate in the early church whose progress is given in unusual detail. Though often called the first Council of Jerusalem, it bears little resemblance to the great ecumenical councils that followed (Nicea, Constantinople, Trent, etc.). It bears equally little resemblance to a democratic vote. The final decision involved consultation between leaders, sharing experience, frank discussion, relating spiritual conviction, searching for God's recognisable blessing, and expounding and interpreting the Scriptures.

THEORY TURNED TO PRACTICE

How should a church meeting function?

Godly people. It should consist of people known to have a spiritual commitment. Ideally, it should not be announced for a special time weeks in advance (which is an invitation to normal non-attenders at prayer and Bible study to flock along). Rather it should be held at a time when Christians normally gather for other spiritual exercises...the special business being added simply because various matters have arisen. Does the church still follow the older pattern of centralised midweek meeting for Bible study and prayer? Many still do. In that case, a half hour of business could be added to that exercise when necessary. Members who are unwilling to give themselves to their local church's normal pattern of church discipline are not very obviously qualified to step into its occasional decision making. If on the other hand the church has a network of house groups rather than a centralised midweek meeting, then the groups could be called together when decisions are to be made. Alternatively (or as well) the members could be asked to stay after the Lord's Supper to attend to church business. This would be particularly appropriate for reporting on applicants for membership, planning evangelism, making adjustments to public worship, etc.

Trusted Leadership. When a rather more local problem cropped up in the early church (favouritism and jealousy in the widows' soup kitchen), the top leaders said in effect, 'Appoint second-line leaders of your own choice, making sure they are spiritual men, and then trust them to get on with it' (Acts 6:1–6). The congregation did so. Indeed they expressed a remarkable degree of trust, for in a quarrel in which the Hellenistic members felt shabbily treated by the Hebrews, the unanimous decision was to appoint seven men with Hellenistic names.

Leaders are appointed to lead. Deacons bringing back to a hundred members a request for a decision on which colour to paint the schoolroom are either dodging their responsibility or are not being given any. Leaders who decide to conduct a major evangelistic mission without ever asking the members would be going to the opposite extreme.

Searching the Scriptures. There is something odd and sad about a church meeting at which the minute book and the rule book are prominent and oft-consulted whilst the Bible lies unopened and unquoted. Church business should be accompanied, not merely by the token reading of a 'suitable scripture' at the beginning, but by the searching of the Bible. Acknowledged teachers (ordained or lay) should be able to guide the members and be listened to. That is why a meeting called exclusively for business, separate from the weekly time for devotion and Bible study, is really starting off on the wrong foot.

Praying together. This should not be a mere conventional start to the proceedings (hymn, psalm, reading, minutes of the last meeting ... now then, the real nitty-gritty!). It was when leaders were already at prayer that they became conscious of a missionary call; when the church was deeply in prayer that the answer to a crisis was given (Acts 12:1–17; 13:1–4). The business meeting should surely be a *prayer meeting*. I wish I had had the courage to make a bid for church meetings attended only by supporters of the weekly prayer meeting or its household equivalents!

Finding a common mind. I have always regarded 'putting it to a vote' as something of a measure of failure — unless in circumstances where a free *and secret* expression of opinion is essential (the final decision as to whether to call a certain pastor, for example — clearly no one should be inhibited or influenced by the fear of being branded as 'against the new man.') At both leadership and membership level, it should be possible to sense a consensus, to be aware of the people finding God's will through prayer, Bible guidance, open discussion, suggestions, exchange of information. If that consensus does not emerge, I would hesitate to move forward in a certain direction—unless indeed those opposed to it were notoriously the same 'no-change-at-any-price' people, (precisely what they often are). Hence a secret ballot is often of little value. We want to assess the objections and the track record of those who make them. I have seen (and been happy to see) a decision put off or altered because someone godly who rarely speaks, or who normally goes along with the suggestions, raises a thoughtful objection. I have also seen a stubborn, immovable problem melt away a month later when I have said, 'Brothers and sisters, we are stuck. Go home and pray about it every day, and we'll meet again next month.' When we have met again in due course everyone has felt the same — or a new unthought factor has cropped up that made the decision for us.

At best a kind of semi-vote would be helpful. I might say, 'This is not a ballot. We are not undertaking to be bound by the figures in this vote. But we need to be more clear about the general feeling here, and many of you are saying nothing. Please indicate by a show of hands who is happy about this suggestion.... Thank you. Who is hesitant about it?... Thank you. Now I believe the elders should meet again after prayer, bearing that expression in mind, and bring a revised suggestion.' It has worked, again and again.

The people of God exercising discipline. Several scriptures point us to something like the church meeting as the final arbiter in matters of discipline. In the Matthew 18 pattern, this is the last resource when all else has failed. The process does not *begin* there, it ends there if earlier steps of private reproof and leadership guidance do not succeed. Sin or error in the fellowship affects the whole body, so at some stage the whole body needs to become involved. Paul rebuked the whole church at Corinth, to whom his epistle is obviously designed to be read aloud, because they had not dealt with immorality and heresy.

Great care needs to be exercised at this point. Breaking of confidences and public blackening of character must be avoided. This is where the leadership must be trusted.

I recall bringing a name before the church meeting to be struck from the church roll. Christian standards had been abandoned and church attendance had ceased. To some church members this was not quite enough to merit dismissal. Should I share further intimate details, known only to the elders? One wise member made a suggestion which all accepted. 'Make one more personal effort to bring him back, and tell him of our love. If he resists that, strike his name off without giving us further details.' Here was the whole church sharing discipline and exercising the appropriate roles of pastorate, membership and eldership.

Notes

1. Henry Walter, *The Ideal Church*, Carey Publications, 1972.
2. Nigel Wright, 'Is the Church Meeting Dead?' *Mainstream* 15 (January 1984), pp2–4.

CHAPTER FIFTEEN

Unanswered Questions

IT is time to tidy up a few loose ends. Every reader will have his own experiences or anticipated problems which have not been touched on so far. There is no way to have a classified list of rules to cover every contingency. Any attempt to produce it would require something like the Jewish Talmud, which took about three centuries to put together, and requires a lifetime to read with care.

We have something better: the written word of God for our basic principles, and the promise of Christ's guiding presence in his church.

We are in a dynamic, mobile situation, not a static one. Custom, culture, class, contemporary pressures, even the meaning of words, all change and influence our approach to disciplinary problems. We have to remember that God is building a holy people, not a body of legislation.

WHAT OFFENCES MERIT EXCOMMUNICATION?

It is not merely a matter of what particular sin is committed but also of what attitude is taken by the offender, and what effect it has on the church membership and its witness. The Corinthian list, clearly linked with dismissal, includes immorality, greed, idol-worship, slander, drunkenness and thieving (I Corinthians 5:11, and notice the words 'remove the evil man from your group' in verse 13). A similar list in chapter 6 includes legal disputing in a pagan court against a Christian (which Paul regards as robbery), and then the previous list again, with the addition of 'adulterers' and 'homosexual perverts' (verses 7–10). It is a list with some startling implications. Clearly *persistent and defiant practice* is assumed. A man struggling with alcoholism who welcomes help (though with the occasional fall that so often goes with the

145

process) is not a drunkard within this definition. A Christian aware of homosexual tendencies, acknowledging their evil, and seeking deliverance from them, needs counsel and support, not dismissal. Greed implies not just a leaning towards the enjoyment of the good things of life, but a passion for something which thrusts ethical concerns aside and amounts to idolatry. Even put that way, it should give pause for thought to some Christian businessmen! 'Idol-worshipper' is obvious: someone who gives the place which God alone must have to some other being or thing, real or imaginary, cannot remain in the fellowship of God's people. That would include reversion to the religion previously held before conversion, lingering practices definitely linked with that religion (such as recourse to a witch doctor or shaman) and tampering with spiritualism and the occult. Of course, in every case, excommunication is the final resort, not the first.

WHAT OF MINOR OFFENCES?

Immorality, idolatry and heresy are clearly special cases, requiring excommunication. Smaller offences will demand varying steps along that path we have examined, of private admonition, discussion between two or three, elders' action, full church discussion, public warning and withdrawal of Communion.

Where do we draw the line? Martin Luther threatened to excommunicate a man who brought a house for thirty guilders, improved it, and planned to sell it for four hundred. He called that 'barefaced greed,' and cannily suggested that a hundred and fifty would be about right! After all, the Bible has a lot to say about covetousness. House price gazumpers, beware! A derogatory reference to Calvin's Geneva mentions withholding Communion from a widow who said 'rest in peace' at her husband's grave; from a man who wrote a comic song about John Calvin; and from a woman who consulted a fortune teller. That certainly sounds a bit excessive. But examined more closely it leads us to ask what the *motives* of the offenders were. The widow's phrase at that time had connotations of Catholic sympathy in a situation of life and death struggle for the heart of the gospel. Was the comic song a symptom of the hatred which Calvin's Bible teaching stirred up among the carnal? Consulting a fortune teller could well involve rebellion against God's rule and a tampering with the forbidden occult. Attitudes are the key, not mere actions.

The New Testament has some surprising references to minor

discipline which are less surprising if we look at them in this light.

Drunkenness (not merely drinking) was inextricably interwoven with idolatry and sexual excess (Ephesians 5:18; I Timothy 3:3).

The *laziness* at Thessalonica was not merely a matter of being work shy. It went with an excessive and unbalanced fashion for fulfilled prophecy which said, 'Jesus is coming back at any minute. Drop everything. Forget your duties. Nothing else matters' (II Thessalonians 2:1–3; 3:6–7, 11–12).

Persistent *quarrelling* had two features which threatened the early church's situation. It sprang from foolish religious speculation in opposition to biblical truth. It cast a shadow over that loving fellowship which was such an evangelistic attraction (Romans 16:17).

Dishonesty showed itself in a special form precisely because other people's generosity and sacrifice were making a powerful impact (Acts 4:32—5:11).

It is doubtful whether we can make a kind of legal code for church discipline. So often it is the personal attitude and the local situation which are the deciding factors.

REBELLION AGAINST THE PASTOR

Yes it happens! Sometimes he deserves it and sometimes not. However it happens, it is always a bad sign of breakdown somewhere. The vicar of the established church is often in a special position, with regard both to the legal power of his incumbency and the authority of the bishop who stands behind him. The Nonconformist pastor still has some protection in a 'presbyterian' system (whether it be Elim Pentecostal, house church or United Reformed). The protection in each case also brings responsibility and submission.

In the 'independent' system, the pastor is terribly vulnerable. He also has enormous freedom to win and hold leadership by his spiritual and moral qualities alone. Independent churches need to think hard about 'higher' protection of the pastor. The Baptist Union system of Superintendents moving amongst self-governing churches has many virtues, as has their newer system of additional area ministers.

If he is attacked, the pastor must try to establish the real motive. Is his stand for *fundamental truth* under fire? He should have made sure long before the trouble began that he has some statement of faith to fall back on. 'This is what you called me to teach' should be his defence. Here an eldership is essential (whatever its precise name). If *they* think he is wrong, then either he is, or the whole church is pretty hopelessly in error. He should think of moving — or (more likely?) he should look again at the balance of what he is teaching, and the speed at which he is expecting to be followed.

There are differences of emphasis within fundamental truth, about which the pastor must be honest from the beginning. It does not seem to me to be honest to come to a church secretly determined to 'push' the doctrine of election, or open communion, or 'baptism in the Spirit', but hiding that fact from the officers and members. If the pastor's convictions change in the course of a pastorate, he should be honest about that too; *not* by dramatically announcing it from the unanswerable safety of the pulpit but by sharing frankly with leaders and members in the Matthew 18 atmosphere of discussion, fellowship and prayer. I recall how nervously I approached a deacons' meeting when I had become almost reluctantly aware of a quiet healing ministry. To my relief and joy their attitude was open, sympathetic and encouraging, whilst a little cautious and warning 'Let's see what God does,' they said. We saw. If the pastor has to resort to the pulpit as the place to defend himself, the struggle is probably lost already.

Wise and godly advice from outside should be sought. Inside the whirlpool it is difficult to look objectively. A more objective view may be found in your denominations ministers' fraternal, your local clergy fraternal, advice from a colleague from another church, or consultation with your superintendent.

A minister should not permit a personal verbal attack on himself or his officers in a public gathering. No system I have ever heard of can justify that. He should close the meeting and make the attacker take the course commended in Matthew 18. Ultimately, God has his own stern ways of dealing with the form of rebellion against leadership that is really rebellion against himself.

MORAL ACCUSATION AGAINST A LEADER

The Bible puts this in a special category: 'Do not listen to an accusation against an elder unless it is brought by two or more witnesses' (I Timothy 5:19). Why? Because a Christian leader is in a special position of vulnerability. He is exposed to Satan's attacks because of his front-line position. His work necessarily leads him into dangerous and delicate moral issues. Pastoral counselling creates special perils.

'Transference' is a phenomenon familiar to secular counsellors and psychiatrists. The person receiving deep and intimate counselling can turn affection, or need, or perversion on to the counsellor. Through genuine emotional sickness, through hysteria, through deliberate malice, or through resentment of the advice given, the patient can fall in love with the pastor, or become obsessed with him, or come to hate him, or imagine a romantic relationship with him, or fantasise in various ways, or simply tell convincing lies. There can be a demonic element too.

For years now I have made it a personal rule never to counsel a woman or girl alone in the house or in an empty church. When it has been totally unavoidable in a heavy ministry, I have ensured that my pastoral appointments were in a diary and that my wife or members of the pastoral team knew about each one. It is possible to counsel in a vestry with the door partly open and the caretaker or someone working nearby in the building. I would only counsel a wife with her husband's consent, or, if in some very unusual situation that was impossible, then with another woman present.

This kind of caution has saved me from some nasty moments — like a disturbed girl who began to undress, and a prostitute who pretended to be an enquirer in order to blacken my name. Whilst believing in the scriptural laying on of hands and the biblical 'holy kiss,' I would be very reluctant to share either in a one-to-one situation! Happy the minister who has a pastoral team or eldership with whom he can share his counselling appointments (without breaking confidences) and know he is being prayed for at that time.

A leader is vulnerable for other reasons, too. He will be popular amongst grateful people who openly admire him. A woman he has helped may show him more affection and admiration than his own wife shows (he has a foolish wife in that case, but it happens). In his enthusiasm for the fascinating work, he can give more attention to another woman than to his own wife (now he is the foolish one). One brings her problems by appointment half way through an interesting day; the other is waiting with them at the tail-end of a tiring day. Somehow it is not at all the same!

From observation I would estimate that serious falls amongst leaders are commonly connected with sex, money or pride. Augustine's motto was:

> Towards my God, a heart of fire;
> towards my neighbour, a heart of love;
> towards myself, a heart of steel.

HOW PERSONAL SHOULD MORAL TEACHING AND CENSURE BE?

If we are handling the Word of God, under the anointing of the Holy Spirit, the need for actually naming people should be rare. God has a way of applying his word! The Greek scholar A.T. Robertson wrote an article on *Diotrophes* (he 'likes to be their leader', III John 9–10) in a magazine for Christian leaders, and twenty deacons from various churches cancelled their subscriptions because of 'personal attacks' made on them in the article though no personalities appeared in it! I once prayed in the public intercessions for God to deal with any back-biting, position-seeking and jealousy there might be amongst us. I intended it in quite general terms, but a member angrily upbraided me for 'getting personal' about him and several of his friends. Obviously God was stirring consciences!

LEGAL ENTANGLEMENTS

The American scene has produced a shocking new complication, with the news of several church members taking their leadership to court for character defamation in the pursuit of church discipline. It is shocking, because the resource they have claimed is clearly forbidden in Scripture.

> If one of you has a dispute with a fellow-Christian, how dare he go before heathen judges instead of letting God's people settle the matter? ... The very fact that you have legal disputes among yourselves shows that you have failed completely.
>
> I Corinthians 6:1–7

I gather that litigation has a great fascination for the African mind, too. If a church leadership is attacked in this way, the injunction seems to be to turn the other cheek, and at the most simply state the facts. 'Would it not be better for you to be wronged?' (verse 7).

There is nothing wrong in taking precautionary action in the first place, to avoid certain dangers. Churches in future may need to incorporate into their reception of members a signed statement of willingness to be disciplined on scriptural grounds. This could include brief biblical references (say, Matthew 18:15–20; I Corinthians 5:1–13; Galatians 6:1; II Thessalonians 3:14–15; I Timothy 5:19–20; I Corinthians 6:1–8). Leaders should also be very careful not to break pastoral confidences, not to report the issues outside their own local fellowship, and not to get involved in harassment or the inflicting of emotional distress. A church meeting (or its equivalent) should be willing, if necessary, to accept a recommendation of the leadership for discipline without needing to know all the personal details. If they are not willing to, they cannot really have leaders. Care should be taken in replying to a request from another church to receive the transfer of a member 'under discipline.' It might be wise, for example, to reply, 'In the light of this church's understanding of church discipline, it would be difficult for us to give a whole-hearted recommendation.'

PROBLEMS WITH SPIRITUAL GIFTS

This is not the place for a review and critique of the charismatic movement. I simply recognise that some problems of church discipline are raised by renewal.

The divided church.   There may be serious differences of opinion within a local church on the nature, number and use of spiritual gifts. They should be resolved by recourse to the Word of God, by open and honest sharing of views, and in an atmosphere of love and respect, not of suspicion and intolerance. If one opinion is based on the assumption that charismata are from the devil, or another starts with the assumption that all traditionalists are carnal or dead, there is little prospect of understanding. One-sided tales from other churches should not dominate the discussion. Members should accord each other the respect of actually listening to what they are saying.

A few facile slogans should be dismissed.

'Open worship' is undoubtedly found in the New Testament, *but it is not the only kind*; liturgical, and free-but-structured forms of worship are equally biblical.

Charismata need not be exclusively linked with open worship.

It is facile to say that the Holy Spirit never causes division, so anything that divides cannot be from the Holy Spirit. In fact the Holy Spirit has often caused division by highlighting truth — as in the Protestant Reformation, the formation of the Free Churches, and the growth of evangelicalism. The question is, who precipitates the division, and why? In my observation, charismatics and traditionalists are about equally guilty. The member who avers, 'If anyone speaks in tongues I shall walk out', is a divider as much as the member who says, 'If I feel excited I shall speak in tongues no matter whom it hurts or upsets.'

Another facile slogan is, 'the Holy Spirit is the Spirit of truth, therefore he will never teach something which I do not believe' (which is what people often mean when they say, 'therefore he will never teach error'!).

Belief in the spiritual gifts does *not* have to go hand-in-hand with a second-blessing baptism-in-the-Spirit theology (which of course is bound by its nature to be divisive). A wise pastor will rejoice when his people relate spiritual experiences to him, and then steer them into a better biblical understanding of them.

Belief in the charismata may well go with a discovery of church-growth principles. It may arise simply from a confrontation with a situation in which hitherto unfamiliar gifts are seen to be needed. None of this need cause a panicky belief that Pentecostalism is taking over.

Pastor and leaders should be able to expect that a renewing work of the Holy Spirit will deepen the respect of members for their spiritual leaders, and strengthen their willingness to receive biblical advice.

Sometimes, sadly, division may be unavoidable. If so, it should be arranged without rancour, without involving personalities, and in the recognition that two groups of sincere Christians may find it impossible to work together structurally, and yet respect each other as fellow Christians seeking to obey the one Lord. I would take a lot of persuading that the takeover of a reluctant church by renewal enthusiasts over the heads, or behind the backs, of established leaders is ever justified. Better to part friends and serve the Lord separately but in mutual love. I gather that a major influence in the phenomenal growth of churches in Latin America is their tendency to subdivide over quite small matters of personality or policy. Division can sometimes be multiplication!

MISUSE OF GIFTS

A church may welcome a full use of spiritual gifts, and yet find problems with their misuse. Emotional people may dominate the worship, with what is simply an excess of feeling. Someone with a grudge may work it off by 'prophesying' against the leaders. Wild claims for blanket healing based on dubious theology may cause distress. Leaders have a special responsibility to 'test the spirits'. In my observation, really successful 'charismatic' churches (of whatever denomination) are invariably churches with strong leaders who can be very firm indeed about what is permitted and who does what!

Paul's words to Corinth and Thessalonica are as relevant today as they were in the first century:

> It is one and the same Spirit who does all this; as he wishes, he gives a different gift to each person.
>
> I Corinthians 12:11

> Set your hearts, then, on the more important gifts. Best of all, however, is the following way … love.
>
> I Corinthians 12:31—13:1

> Since you are eager to have the gifts of the Spirit, you must try above everything else to make greater use of those which help to build up the church.
>
> I Corinthians 14:12

> Everything must be done in a proper and orderly way.
>
> I Corinthians 14:40

> Do not restrain the Holy Spirit; do not despise inspired messages. Put all things to the test: keep what is good and avoid every kind of evil.
>
> I Thessalonians 5:19

THE PROBLEM OF GOSSIP AND SLANDER

It comes as a shock to read that slander is classed with drunkenness, idolatry and gross sexual sins (I Corinthians 5:11–13 and I Corinthians 6:7–10). The remedy is drastic.

> You should not associate with (such) a person.

> Remove the evil man from your group.

> None of these will possess God's Kingdom.

Writing to Thessalonica, Paul seems to have something milder in mind, and simply says, 'Warn them to lead orderly lives' (II Thessalonians 3:12). It is a sobering reflection. Alongside 'judging,' gossip is almost the characteristic vice of many evangelical communities.

I take 'slander' to be the deliberate assassination of character with a malicious intention, whilst 'gossip' usually has a more innocent intention and springs from the constitutional inability of some people to hold their tongues.

Why is slander such a serious offence? First it is precisely the kind of vice which always requires discipline in the New Testament. It disrupts church community life inside, and ruins its witness outside. I recall a man whose Christian commitment was delayed for years, although he regulaly attended my church. He gave as one reason for hesitation the conversation of well-established church members who sat next to him in the congregation. They whiled away the twenty-minute wait by analysing, in loud whispers, the dress, appearance and recent record of everyone who came through the door, the character of every deacon and steward who came on duty, and the dubious intentions of the minister as read between the lines of the printed announcements. Cheerfully ignorant of the harm they were doing, they might just as well have heckled the preacher or handed out atheistic leaflets!

Second, it is impossible to build a loving, caring and trusting fellowship if its members cannot control their comments about the discovered frailties of their fellow members. Building community life is a sensitive business (some churches don't even attempt it). Broken people are mended slowly. Foolish gossip can bring down a painfully built structure of trust in a few hours.

I recall the new convert who was extraordinarily ashamed of his colour blindness. A member of a nurture group of new converts with many painful memories of past vices abandoned, he eventually admitted it in confidence — very much as if he was confessing to leprosy or meths drinking. Within a day his confidante had shared the fascinating news (in confidence, of course) with two others, who each told two more. We nearly lost a family, and the members of the group disbanded and joined other groups. They simply felt that trust had gone.

Third, Satan himself uses slander with great effect. It is a favourite weapon of his. The devil is characteristically the slanderer, 'the one who ... accused our brothers day and night' (Revelation 12:10). The passage is fascinating, for it shows us where the victory lies — 'by the blood of the Lamb and by the truth which they proclaimed' (verse 11). Christ has shed his blood for those sins and offences of which Satan (and some church members) accuse the believer. The complete atonement and ongoing intercession of Jesus ('the blood of the Lamb') combine with the truth announced, enforced and applied, of the reconciling Gospel and the reconciled community ('the truth which they proclaimed') — there is the answer to Satan's accusations.

154

Fourth, careless and critical talk spreads poison. James, the Lord's brother, gives a devastating picture of its effect.

> How large a forest can be set on fire by a tiny flame! And the tongue is like a fire. It is a world of wrong, occupying its place in our bodies and spreading evil through our whole being.
>
> James 3:5–6

Significantly, the writer sets the whole passage in the context of teaching and leadership (verses 1–3).

Insidious influence is the fifth danger of slander and gossip. Semi-anonymous and behind the scenes, it is hard to track down and to combat. One painful experience led me to establish a simple rule at leadership level. Never accept an anonymous charge, and never bring to the eldership issues passed on 'in confidence' by someone who wishes to remain unknown. An officer forced through the eldership a reluctant confrontation with the leaders of one of the church departments — on the say-so of a member whose identity he would not reveal. The leaders were totally innocent, and we had to help them to produce a written constitution to defend them from any more accusations.

So often an elder or similar leader can become the unwitting cat's-paw of a troublemaker.

'People are not happy about last Sunday's evening service,' he will announce. 'They say it was too emotional (dull, noisy, quiet, long, or short).'

'Which people?' I would ask.

'Well, they spoke privately to me — I don't think I can mention names.'

'Then I'm sorry, but you can't mention the opinions either,' I would reply. 'We have no way to assess the value of the opinion if we know nothing of the person who expresses it. Is it a regular troublemaker? A mature member? A thoughtful observer? A fanatic with a hobbyhorse to ride?'

Anonymous letters create a similar problem, of course. I look immediately for the signature on any letter I receive. If it is signed, 'Concerned Church Member', 'Well-wisher' or 'A Friend,' it goes unread into the wastepaper basket. Just sometimes, I wonder what I have missed!

The final danger I suggest is that slander undermines the whole principle of pastoral care and trusted leadership on which a church is built. Confidentiality is absolutely essential for pastoral care and counselling. If that is to be maintained, the onlookers will often see the pastoral advice worked out, *but be ignorant of the full facts behind it.*

'The present eldership doesn't take the Bible line on divorce and remarriage,' said a member sweepingly on the telephone to me. What she really meant was that the elders had given advice on several delicate matters, *the facts of which she did not know*. To have shared those facts would have been to ensure that no one else in need brought their problems to that eldership.

How can these offences be dealt with?   Regular teaching should be given on the subject. There is no shortage of biblical material! Foolish and unintentional gossip merits a pastoral visit, a gentle rebuke, and sometimes the offer of help to the offender, for often it springs from boredom, loneliness, disappointment, and the need to be noticed. This is surely what II Thessalonians 3:12 is advocating.

Deliberate and malicious slander should be handled according to the pattern of Matthew 18. There should be a particular emphasis on being accompanied by a witness. Needless to say, slander at a public meeting should be silenced instantly, even if it is presented in an elaborately constitutional and precedural manner, or proposed as a question. If public harm is done by slander, then public rebuke and public recantation are in order. Persistent and deliberate continuation in slander, after private, semi-private and public warning, merits expulsion. One might almost label the expulsion exorcism!

Does that sound a little like going over the top? Then reflect on this simple fact. The word *diabolos*, used thirty-four times in the New Testament as the title of Satan ('the devil'), is also used as 'slanderer' or 'false accuser' for those who cause trouble in the church by attacking the characters of other members (I Timothy 3:11; II Timothy 3:3; Titus 2:3).

EPILOGUE

Shaped or Spineless?

ENGLISH nursery rhymes are curious creations. They are full of veiled social, political and religious comment whose meaning has been long forgotten. Who now recalls 'Little Jack Horner'? He was an unpopular ingratiate of King Charles, who pulled a plum job out of his royal patronage. 'Mary, Mary, quite contrary' was the Catholic Queen Mary who enraged her Protestant subjects by burning martyrs, including 'pretty maids all in a row.' The innocent children's game 'Ring-a-roses' is a grim race memory of the terrible Plague, which was heralded by rose-coloured blotches on the skin, could not be warded off by a 'pocket full of posies' (sweet-smelling herbs) and reached a stage marked by violent sneezing followed swiftly by death — 'Atishoo, atishoo, we all fall down.'

Some of the rhymes contain very pointed pastoral advice. Who was the 'boy who looks after the sheep'? Whoever he was, he didn't do his job properly, for he was 'under the haycock, fast asleep.' He was certainly *not* looking after them, for a shepherd's job is a sleeples task. Neglect them, and they wander off. Fall asleep on duty and you may never see them again. Totally inappropriate is the advice given to 'Little Bo-peep' who 'lost her sheep and didn't know where to find them.' What was the advice? 'Leave them alone, and they'll come home, wagging their tails behind them.' But they won't. Sheep left alone don't wander home, they wander away. The Bible is full of warnings to that effect. Some of the sharpest warnings in Old and New Testament alike are directed at shepherds who don't do their job. A quick check through a concordance is a sobering experience.

You shepherds of Israel! You ... never tend the sheep....
You have not taken care of the weak ones,
   healed those that are sick,

157

bandaged those that are hurt,
brought back those that wandered off,
or looked for those that were lost.

Ezekiel 34:2–4

When the hired man, who is not a shepherd and does not own the sheep, sees a wolf coming, he leaves the sheep and runs away; so the wolf snatches the sheep and scatters them.

John 10:12

Shepherding includes discipline. The rod and the staff bring comfort — eventually. Hooked through the sheep's wool to pull him from danger, pushing the sheep forward when he is reluctant to move, they shepherd with sternness for the better welfare of the sheep.

It is the least pleasant part of shepherding, but it must be done. Apologetic leadership, pseudo-democratic consensus and the shirking of painful responsibility have brought the church in the West to a sorry state.

Let us change the metaphor. Discipline has been called the backbone of the church. A spineless body has trouble standing up — for anything. We see a Christendom ashamed of the Gospel, apologetic about the fundamentals of sound doctrine, hesitant to make an unpopular moral stand, and wringing its hands helplessly at the misbehaviour and meandering of its members. Only when the scandal reaches the verge of the ridiculous do we stop and consdier where we are going: gay churches with homosexual marriage services; theologians who teach that God is dead; clergy who organise séances; bishops who give cheerful assent to a creed — as long as, like Alice's Humpty Dumpty, they can reserve the right to make the words mean whatever they wish them to mean. Members who take their elders to court for obeying Christ's injunction to bring misdemeanours to the church. And so on.

The church that fails to exercise discipline will lose its self-respect and the respect of others. The church is called to dispense salt, not honey, says Helmut Thielicke. When it does that,

… the world will have to reckon with you.
Corruption will be slowed and reversed by you.
The world won't like it, but can't ignore it.

WHAT IS CHURCH DISCIPLINE?

It is the serious attempt to preserve the truth, order and standards of New Testament Christianity in the local church. It is the determination to take the Son of God seriously, and to hearken to his apostles. It is designed for the preservation of spiritual life, the authentication of the church's witness, the discouragement of sin, and the restoration of the fallen. We preserve our spiritual life by doing our best to ensure that membership is only for the spiritually alive. We authenticate our witness by proclaiming scriptural truth and living lives that illustrate its power. We discourage sin by making sure not only that our teaching deplores it but that our inaction does not condone it. We restore the fallen, not by leading them to suppose from our silence that their fall does not matter, but by showing them its consequences and pulling them back from the brink.

I raised a question of possible discipline in my home church with a fine leader of evangelism and church planting in Europe. Should I tackle it, or let it rest? As we sped in his car along an autobahn, he reply was brief and blunt: 'If you never do any weeding, the garden will be strangled.'

The movement he serves is planting brave little churches in a hostile environment. It is finding eager young recruits for voluntary evangelism, in tough conditions, in minimum comfort, where emotional attachments are avoided until the task is done. There is no shortage of recruits, for genuine challenge does not frighten away the committed. His is a fairly small movement. I know another, vastly bigger, working worldwide, perhaps the most significant missionary thrust of the third quarter of this century. It is not a wing of the house church movement. It shows no signs of cult tendences. Its birth preceded that of the charismatic movement. It displays some of the characteristics of the early Franciscans, the original Moravians, the first Wesleyans. Whilst lowest-common-denominator movements are declining, highest-common-factor movements like this flourish. The young will certainly not shrink from it if they have a glimpse of Jesus.

> Christ the Son of God has sent me
> To the midnight lands
> Mine the mighty ordination
> Of the pierced hands.

I once feared that my own sons would be put off Christianity by the comparative poverty involved in being a pastor's son in England (where Wesley's words, 'the humble poor believe,' find new meaning; we learn to accept cheerfully and with good humour that God keeps us believing, the congregation keeps us poor, and the deacons keep us humble!). In actual fact both of them (now adult) set lifestyles for themselves which are radical in their simplicity, regarding few possessions as really necessary, giving tithes and offerings and more with a breathtaking insouciance, and at times seeming to suspect that dear old dad and mum have become a shade too comfortable and worldly in their declining years! This is an attitude to discipleship taken by many of our younger Christians. There is no fear that they will wince away from a vision, a commitment and a discipline that is Christ-centred and Spirit-motivated.

Where I work in Jerusalem, a couple of sixth-formers approached me (boy and girl, hand-in-hand) as young Israelis who wanted the interesting experience of talking to a Christian. 'What are you studying at school?' I asked the boy.

'Oh, I left school a few weeks ago; I drive a tank in Lebanon,' he replied casually.

I see them everywhere; 'courting couples,' we would have called them, strolling with arms around each other's waists in the golden Jerusalem sunshine. It is a boy-and-girl's army that makes the Middle East tremble. As they stroll, the boy carries a sub-machine gun and the girl a rifle.

They do it willingly, for an earthly vision of Zionistic idealism. Need we assume that our Christian youth in a new day of church growth want to be any less committed, aggressive, vigilant, disciplined and mobilised, for the heavenly Jerusalem and the Commander of Kings?

Someone has said that ethics is love in working clothes. Perhaps we can add that discipline is love in armour.

The Mustard Seed Conspiracy

by Tom Sine

The Mustard Seed Conspiracy could change your life. It invites you to a celebration and an adventure.

'God wants to use your life to make a difference in his world,' writes Tom Sine. The glorious tomorrow God has promised us has already begun, and we are invited to be part of it.

To those who feel that the world's problems are too great to tackle, Dr Sine offers a way forward. A professional student of future trends, he sets out some of the challenges we are likely to face in the next two decades, then shows how we can find God's clear direction as we explore creative responses to these opportunities. His powerful arguments are studded with practical examples — *Mustard Seeds* — from across the world of how God is already working for change through his people.

'Compelling ... combines solid biblical theology with solid futures study.' *Ronald Sider*

'"Must" reading for those who want to make a difference.'
Jay Kesler, President, Youth for Christ International

4 Million Reasons to Care

by David Porter and Peter Elsom

The authors offer an intensely practical, clear analysis — in 'lay' terms — of the present unemployment situation. Concentrating on the resources of the 53,000 churches in the UK, they show how Christians — and others — can fight unemployment in their own neighbourhood. Realistic, original, clear-headed: here are ideas that work.

Published jointly with Church Action with the Unemployed

Meditative Prayer

by Richard Foster

A brief, powerful account of the essentials of meditative prayer.

'Jesus Christ is alive and here to teach his people himself. His voice is not hard to hear; his vocabulary is not hard to understand. But we must learn how to hear his voice and to obey his word.'

In meditative prayer, writes Richard Foster, we find that the presence of the Lord moves from a theological dogma into a radiant reality. We create the emotional and spiritual space which allows Christ to construct an inner sanctuary in the heart.

Your Spiritual Gifts Can Help Your Church Grow
How to Find Your Gift and Use It

by Peter Wagner

Discover the spiritual gifts God intends you to exercise within the Body of Christ.

Why another book on spiritual gifts? Many eagerly seek spiritual gifts, but Peter Wagner argues that gifts are not an end in themselves, but a means to an end — to enable Christians to obey Christ's command to make disciples of all nations.

'This is essentially a book on church health. Churches grow because they are healthy. Therefore, developing the dynamic of spiritual gifts in a church — because it is biblical and because it will enhance the health of the Body — should also help churches to grow.'

The author demonstrates that gifts are not just to increase numbers, but to promote wholeness. Examining each gift in detail, he shows how the gifts can become operative in your church now.

Dr Wagner has been Vice-President of the Fuller Evangelistic Association and Associate Professor of Church Growth at the Fuller Theological Seminary School of World Mission since 1971. A former missionary to Bolivia for 15 years, Dr Wagner is author of more than a dozen books.

Ten Growing Churches

by Eddie Gibbs

All over the United Kingdom churches are growing.

Here are ten churches, from different areas and denominations, which are seeing their congregations grow and mature.

Eddie Gibbs, who has conducted many Church Growth courses for Bible Society, has chosen ministers from the Anglican, Church of Scotland, Methodist, Baptist, United Reformed, Elim, Free Evangelical and the House Churches. They come from the inner city, suburbia, industrial and rural areas. Together they offer a range of encouraging models, illustrating how God is at work in *ordinary* churches today.

With honesty and courage each has described both successes and failures. There are no checklists or patterns to be slavishly followed — but here is evidence, often dramatic, of God present in power.

Eddie Gibbs is author of several books including *I Believe in Church Growth*. He has recently moved to Pasadena, California, to become Assistant Professor of Church Growth at Fuller Theological Seminary.

Published jointly with the British Church Growth Association.

Laughter in Heaven

Edited by Murray Watts

Five authors have contributed sketches and a full-length morality play to bring the Christian message through drama. Designed to be used in church groups. The writers are all members or associates of the successful Riding Lights Theatre Company based in York.

Says *The Church Times* of their performances at Greenbelt, 'Riding Lights ... are already establishing an enviable reputation for fast humour and slick presentation with a strong Christian voice.'